LEADERSHIP EXCELLENCE IN PROFESSIONAL ADVANCEMENT

DR GAJANAN SHIRKE

This book is dedicated to all Global Leaders

Contents

Acknowledgements

I would like to express a special debt of gratitude to my wife Rajeshree and my two daughters Rupeshi & Kavya, my teammates and superior leaders who encourages me to write.

About Book

Leadership Excellence in Professional Advancement offers the latest managerial trends within the field of management. By collecting research from around the world, in a variety of sectors and levels of technical expertise, this volume offers a broad variety of case studies, best practices, methodologies, and research within the field. The objective of the book is to help professionals in various stages of their careers to hone the key skills that can propel them into success. The following readers will find it very useful:· Leadership s: The skills discussed in this book are universal in nature. The central idca of thc book is to have a consulting mindset for professional success. How can you be more effective in solving your business problems? Reading this book can help you. The book also shares with you career tips, mindsets for success, and ways to overcome career failures and become better every day. These are valuable insights, whether you are junior, a mid-level professional or a senior in your career graph.

About The Author

Dr Gajanan Shirke, a hotel consultant, has years of extensive experience in the hospitality industry. His thirst for learning and aspiration to become a multi-faceted expert in the hotel industry helped him rise from employment to becoming an independent professional in the hospitality sector. Since his last assignment as General Manager at Kamat Hotels, he has become a renowned hotel consultant with a proven track record of developing, training and growing some of the best-known hotels, restaurants and fast-food joints in the Indian market. He was appointed as an expert consultant for The Eighth meeting of the Board of Studies for Hotel Management & Catering Technology. He is a visiting faculty at various Hotel Management Colleges and has trained over a thousand hospitality professionals. He has completed numerous pre and post opening hotel consultancies in India and overseas. In order to spread his extensive knowledge to aspiring hotel professionals, Gajanan has penned a large number of books spanning different segments of the hospitality industry. Starting from his first book 'Bar Management and Operations' published in 2010, he has written 48 books.

Jyotswaroop Singh is entrepreneur headning multinational venture with combined Revenue of US$ 2.25 bn having Having operational offices in London , Singapore , Kampala , Nicosia and Cairo.

Index

CHAPTER ONE

Soft skills you need

Soft skills for leaders are a requirement in today's competitive world, where everyone is striving to go the extra mile to stand out from the crowd. Considering that a lot of employers believe there is a huge skill gap, this doesn't come as surprising. Whatever the case may be, one thing seems clear. Being mediocre isn't enough anymore. Having knowledge in a particular area, and the willingness to go the extra mile to stand out from the crowd is seemingly necessary to get one's foot in the career door.

Soft skills for leaders are the less tangible qualities we all possess. These range from traits that make up our personality, our strengths, our weaknesses, and our attitudes. Skills such as critical thinking, adaptability, and communication, all fall under the umbrella of soft skills. Most of these skills aren't really learned in a classroom but through myriads of everyday experiences. It's critical to understand that no matter how smart or technically proficient you are, your soft skills are what will enable you to truly utilize your knowledge and put your hard skills to use. For example, even a very competent doctor won't be able to keep patients unless he is able to make his patients feel comfortable and put them at ease. Similarly, a businessman with many degrees will probably not be able to close a deal if he doesn't have an approachable personality and isn't able to adapt to a constantly changing business environment.

Empathy and Caring: A leader should really care about his fellow employees. People should feel that the leader thinks "we are all in this together". A real leader should take the time to sit down with their employees to find out what they really want out of life, and more importantly, what motivates them. "People will not care about you as a leader unless they first know you care about them."

Active Listening: A leader should not 'jump in and give solutions, barking out orders. As a leader, you are being paid to 'influence others' and solve - I mean really solve - problems. How do you really know what is at the root of a problem, unless you really actively listen to those involved?

Emotional IQ: The reason most people bring problems and issues to you is often because they feel like they don't have the ability to solve them. A leader should ALWAYS (and I mean ALWAYS) stay 'cool under fire' no matter what the circumstance. I know that's hard sometimes, but if the leader 'blows up' and yells or otherwise belittles his fellow employees every time they come to them with a problem, people will soon stop coming at all - until they can't avoid it -then it always becomes worse.

Public Speaking and Presentation Skills: A good leader will be ready to speak on a wide variety of topics whenever called upon. Leaders should ALWAYS be working on improving these skills. You will NEVER progress in leadership if you don't have the ability to talk well in front of people.

Integrity and Trust: Your people must be able to trust you, even in difficult circumstances. People will NOT take risks if they lack trust in their leadership - the will 'hunker down' and play it safe. Once you have their trust, it's important that you work hard to keep it. I have never seen anyone regain trust in their leaders once it's been broken.

Teamwork: Companies with highly diverse leadership teams make nearly 20% more revenue than those with below-average diversity scores, thereby incentivizing heterogeneity and inclusion. However, the best leaders know that diversity is most valuable when everyone can contribute ideas and collaborate. Because of this, they consciously strive to facilitate teamwork by creating opportunities for cohesion. These same leaders also possess team player characteristics to further encourage cooperation and ensure everyone's voice is heard. For instance, a teamwork-oriented leader might call on soft-spoken individuals to listen to their input. Others might delegate roles and assign responsibilities to each employee so they're productive and committed to achieving results. As the team succeeds and fails together, they'll learn how to better support and motivate each other to accomplish tasks that would have been impossible alone.

Emotional Intelligence: As employees seek more attention through feedback and professional support, leaders must listen closely to truly understand and meet their needs. This soft skill is especially important because it creates trusting relationships in which workers feel empowered to expand their skill sets and further their careers. However, if leaders want to encourage such growth and passion in their employees, they must listen to comprehend rather than simply respond. In other words, they must cultivate emotional intelligence. Emotional intelligence is the ability to perceive, manage and regulate emotions, and it's a key component to active listening. That's because becoming aware of your own feelings teaches you to recognize and influence the feelings of others. Ultimately, this skill can help you resolve conflict, coach and motivate others, and create a collaborative culture where everyone has a chance to succeed.

Communication: Nearly 58% of hiring managers consider communication the most important soft skill for new hires. However, they often forget how integral this ability is to their own job description. Ultimately, how well you communicate thoughts, ideas and solutions will determine your team's level of success. Therefore, you must develop effective writing and speaking skills before trying to convey information to your employees. Maintain eye contact and good posture to show goodwill and project confidence. Avoid fidgeting, and engage your audience through facial expressions and body language. Most importantly, keep speeches to the point. Attention spans are shorter than ever these days, and the last thing you want is for your team to miss any important details. If you can accomplish just as much in an email blast, save time by communicating through writing instead.

Mentoring: More than one-third of people agree that mentors are important, but only 37% have one. Meanwhile, the vast majority of employees are left to fend for themselves. They may never reach their fullest potential without someone to coach them, which is bad news if they're on your team. Luckily, you're in a prime position to fill that mentorship role and help them develop their skills. Make a conscious effort to come alongside your team members and coach them with patience. Allow the mentor-mentee relationship to blossom naturally, and invest in your employees' ongoing learning. Doing so will ensure they become leaders who can assume management responsibilities as the business grows, which will make your job easier in the long run.

Organization: Most leaders are responsible for collecting various resources and datasets, including charts, client information, handouts, reports and other tangible documents. If they're to keep everything in a designated, orderly spot, they must have exceptional organizational skills. Otherwise, they could misplace documents, lose records, and expose sensitive information like payroll histories and credit card data. Leaders must also organize intangible information online. Whether they're collecting productivity reports through a built-in monitoring system or data concerning audience engagement, a number of relevant statistics will end up in a digital file somewhere. It's the leader's job to convert them into more digestible, actionable pieces of information so the team can respond accordingly. More importantly, they'll implement an organizational structure and outline office procedures to maintain a consistent workflow and facilitate a cohesive approach.

Creativity: Leaders understand the importance of rules and regulations. However, the most creative ones realize that some rules are meant to be broken, especially if it means developing better systems and practices. In these instances, they must rely on imagination and ingenuity to formulate and implement creative solutions. Those who truly value inclusivity and growth will involve their team in these creative endeavors, too. Facilitate brainstorming sessions and ask employees to think outside the box. Remember, there are no stupid questions or suggestions in this creative safe space. Besides, spitballing can often lead to brilliant ideas, even if the original concept was a dud. Discuss possible solutions and put them to the test to show everyone you value their recommendations and have faith in their proposals.

Adaptability: Adaptability even during the toughest of times. Of course, most of them had no choice but to alter current systems and make the switch to remote work. However, flexible leaders and their resilient organizations may have had the easiest time of it. Why? Because they were willing to learn, change and grow. In this sense, a leader's adaptability depends on their passion and readiness for improvement and transformation. Are they willing to change the way they've always done things if there's a better solution? More importantly, are they ready to experience setbacks if it means securing success in the long term? Millions of managers asked themselves the same question at the start of the pandemic. Now, only the most adaptable remain.

Problem-Solving: Adaptable leaders often possess excellent problem-solving abilities, too. That's because flexibility demands quick solutions to your most pressing problems. Thus, managers must remain open-minded, lean on transparency and learn to think on their feet. Doing so will help them stay confident in times of crisis so their team can maintain a sense of calm determination and actually instigate change. Approaching and solving office conflict will also help leaders flex their problem-solving muscles. The more often they face opposition, the more easily they can create a framework that will help them resolve it. Using empathy to understand how team members or clients perceive conflict will also allow leaders to practice honing this soft skill.

Decision-Making: When tough decisions arise, leaders are usually the ones who make the final call. Therefore, they must know how to weigh their options and determine the best course of action. This process is much more difficult than it sounds, especially when employees' and clients' comfort and satisfaction often hang in the balance. Plus, each situation may call for a different solution depending on resources, variables and potential outcomes. However, a good, decisive leader knows how to consider all perspectives, analyze relevant data and project possible consequences. After examining the details and the bigger picture, they must choose passivity or action. The latter is typically wisest, even if the decision was a poor one. Then, leaders can learn from their mistakes, adapt and choose a better solution the next time around.

Confidence: Confidence might not seem like a soft skill, especially when so many people find it difficult to cultivate. However, self-confidence is essential for those in leadership, regardless of what industry they work in. That's because confident leaders produce strong and competent followers. When the team perceives their boss to be courageous, innovative and enthusiastic, they'll often exhibit the same characteristics and benefit the entire company. Of course, employers must take care not to become overly confident or arrogant. Otherwise, you may take unreasonable risks and destroy trust among your employees. You might also grow resistant to feedback and personal change, which can hinder growth and prevent your team from achieving results and enjoying success. Therefore, it's best to approach every worker and situation with humility. Then, let confidence inspire others and fuel the problem-solving and decision-making processes.

Now that you know why leaders need soft skills, you may feel inspired to develop your own. While there are many ways to do so, practicing these traits on the job and in real-world situations will help you conquer the learning curve quicker. Expect a few mishaps along the way and use them to hone your skills even further.

CHAPTER TWO

Assertiveness and self Confidence

It is important to know that assertiveness is not a necessity in every area of business. In fact, whilst it may be encouraged in several, there are very few where it would be considered a must have commodity. Too much assertiveness in one workplace can cause arguments and friction, so there must also be people who are just happy getting on with the work. Less assertive people usually have different strengths and get things done in different ways to more confidently spoken people. Very assertive people often favour working with others and expressing their ideas in large groups rather than working on a project on their own. For this reason, quieter people who are happy with no-one else around can often find themselves finishing off others work. Strengths and weaknesses of each type of person help to create a sort of equilibrium in the workplace. Also, when communicating, less assertive people are good at listening to others and taking ideas on board and generally co-operating with their peers.

In terms of self-confidence, whilst this may possibly be considered slightly more of a strength than assertiveness, it can still be of detriment to individuals. For example, people with less confidence tend to get straight to the point when they are speaking due to the fact that they may not be as comfortable partaking in phatic conversation. Less confident people are also often more reliable as they become more concerned about what could happen to them if they, for example, do not hand an assignment in on time. It is important for people who are slightly lacking in self-confidence to realise their strengths and, if they are content with their self-esteem, then getting on with their work in an effective way that works for them. However, if some of you still decide that you would like to boost your assertiveness and self-confidence, there are several ways to do this. Firstly, it is very important for you to know your subject well so that you can have fluent conversations about it with people. Have facts and details relating to the situation to hand. It is also helpful to ask good open questions to keep productive conversations flowing. Finally, be quick and aggressive with your 'trigger responses'. These can give you thinking time and help develop your new persona as a more confident person.

Pure assertiveness – dominance for the sake of being dominant – is not a natural behaviour for most people – the fact is that most people simply are not naturally assertive. The assertive behaviour of highly dominant people tends to be driven by their personality (and often some insecurity). It is not something that has been 'trained'. For anyone seeking to increase their own assertiveness it is helpful to understand the typical personality and motivation of excessively dominant people, who incidentally cause the most worry to non-assertive people.

It's helpful also at this point to explain the difference between leadership with dominance: Good leadership is inclusive, developmental, and a force for what is right. Good leadership does not 'dominate' non-assertive people; it includes them and involves them. Dominance as a management style is not good in any circumstances. It is based on short-term rewards and results, mostly for the benefit of the dominant, and it fails completely to make effective use of team-member's abilities and potential. The fact is that most excessively dominant people are usually bullies. Bullies are deep-down very insecure people. They dominate because they are too insecure to allow other people to have responsibility and influence, and this behaviour is generally conditioned from childhood for one reason or another. The dominant bullying behaviour is effectively reinforced by the response given by 'secure' and 'non-assertive' people to bullying. The bully gets his or her own way. The bullying dominant behaviour is rewarded, and so it persists. Dominant, bullying people, usually from a very young age, become positively conditioned to bullying behaviour, because in their own terms it works. Their own terms are generally concerned with satisfying their ego and selfish drives to get their own way, to control, to achieve status (often implanted by insecure ambitious parents), to manipulate, make decisions, build empires, to collect material signs of achievement, monetary wealth, and particularly to establish protective mechanisms, such as 'yes-men' followers ('body-guards'), immunity from challenge and interference, scrutiny, judgement, etc. Early childhood experiences play an important part in creating bullies. Bullies are victims as well as aggressors. And although it's a tough ask for anyone on the receiving end of their behaviour they actually deserve sympathy.

Non-assertive people do not normally actually aspire to being excessively dominant people and they certainly don't normally want to become bullies. When most people talk about wanting to be more assertive, what they really mean is 'I'd like to be more able to resist the pressure and dominance of excessively dominant people.' Doing this is not really so hard and using the simple techniques above it can even be quite enjoyable and fulfilling. Importantly, the non-assertive person should understand where they really are – a true starting point: non-assertive behaviour is a sign of strength usually, not weakness, and often it is the most appropriate behaviour for most situations – don't be fooled into thinking that you always have to be more assertive.

Understand where you want to be: what level of assertiveness do you want? Probably to defend yourself, and to control your own choices and destiny (which are relatively easy using the techniques below), not to control others. For people who are not naturally assertive, it is possible to achieve a perfectly suitable level of assertiveness through certain simple methods and techniques, rather than trying to adopt a generally more assertive personal style (which could be counter-productive and stressful, because it would not be natural). People seeking to be more assertive can dramatically increase their effective influence and strength by using just one or two of these four behaviours prior to, or when confronted by a more dominant character or influence, or prior to and when dealing with a situation in which they would like to exert more control. Here are some simple techniques and methods for developing self-confidence and more assertive behaviour.

Assertiveness and self-confidence methods and techniques

1. Know your facts and have them to hand.
2. Anticipate other people's behaviour and prepare your responses.
3. Prepare and use good open questions.
4. Re-condition and practice your own new reactions to aggression (display positive writings where you will read them often – it's a proven successful technique).
5. Have faith that your own abilities and style will ultimately work if you let them.
6. Feel sympathy for bullies – they actually need it.

7. Read inspirational things that reinforce your faith in proper values and all the good things in your own natural style and self, for example, Desiderata, Nelson Mandela's inaugural speech, Kipling's If : you will have memorable quotes and sayings of your own...) know your facts and have them to hand

Ensure you know all the facts in advance – do some research, and have it on hand ready to produce (and give out copies if necessary). Bullies usually fail to prepare their facts; they dominate through bluster, force and reputation. If you know and can produce facts to support or defend your position it is unlikely that the aggressor will have anything prepared in response. When you know that a situation is going to arise, over which you'd like to have some influence, prepare your facts, do your research, do the sums, get the facts and figures, solicit opinion and views, be able to quote sources; then you will be able to make a firm case, and also dramatically improve your reputation for being someone who is organised and firm.

The difference between leadership with dominance:

- Good **leadership** is inclusive, developmental, and a force for what is right. Good leadership does not 'dominate' non-assertive people, it includes them and involves them.
- **Dominance** as a management style is not good in any circumstances. It is based on short-term rewards and results, mostly for the benefit of the dominant, and it fails completely to make effective use of team members' abilities and potential.

Dominant People: The fact is that most excessively dominant people are usually bullies. Bullies are deep-down very insecure people. They dominate because they are too insecure to allow other people to have responsibility and influence, and this behaviour is generally conditioned from childhood for one reason or another. The dominant bullying behaviour is effectively reinforced by the response given by 'secure' and 'non-assertive' people to bullying. The bully gets his or her own way. The bullying dominant behaviour is rewarded, and so it persists.

- Dominant, bullying people, usually from a very young age, become positively conditioned to bullying behaviour because in their own terms it works.

- Their own terms are generally concerned with satisfying their ego and selfish drives to get their own way, control, achieve status (often implanted by insecure ambitious parents), manipulate, make decisions, build empires, collect material signs of achievement, monetary wealth, and particularly to establish protective mechanisms, such as 'yes-men' followers ('body-guards'), immunity from challenge and interference, scrutiny, judgment, etc.
- Early childhood experiences play an important part in creating bullies. Bullies are victims as well as aggressors. And although it's a tough challenge for anyone on the receiving end of their behaviour they actually deserve sympathy.

Non-Assertive People: Do not normally actually aspire to be excessively dominant people, and they certainly don't normally want to become bullies.

- When most people talk about wanting to be more assertive, what they really mean is 'I'd like to be more able to resist the pressure and dominance of excessively dominant people.' Doing this is not really so hard, and using simple techniques it can even be quite enjoyable and fulfilling.

Importantly, the non-assertive person should understand where they really are - a true starting point: non-assertive behaviour is a sign of strength usually, not weakness, and often it is the most appropriate behaviour for most situations - don't be fooled into thinking that you always have to be more assertive.

- Understand where you want to be: *what level of assertiveness do you want?* Probably to defend yourself, and to control your own choices and destiny (which are relatively easy using the techniques below), not to control others.

For people who are not naturally assertive, it is possible to achieve a perfectly suitable level of assertiveness through certain simple methods and techniques, rather than trying to adopt a generally more assertive personal style (which could be counter-productive and stressful, because it would not be natural).

- People seeking to be more assertive can dramatically increase their effective influence and strength by using just one or two of these four behaviours prior to, or when confronted by a more dominant character or influence, or prior to and when dealing with a situation in which they would like to exert more control.

Methods and Techniques to become more Assertive

1. Know the facts relating to the situation and have the details to hand.
2. Be ready for - anticipate - other people's behaviour and prepare your responses.
3. Prepare and use good open questions.
4. Re-condition and practice your own new reactions to aggression (posters can help you think and become how you want to be - display positive writings where you will read them often - it's a proven successful technique).
5. Have faith that your own abilities and style will ultimately work if you let them.
6. Feel sympathy for bullies - they actually need it.
7. Read inspirational things that reinforce your faith in proper values and all the good things in your own natural style and self,

Anticipate other people's behaviour and prepare your responses

Anticipate other people's behaviour and prepare your own responses. Role-play in your mind how things are likely to happen. Prepare your responses according to the different scenarios that you think could unfold. Prepare other people to support and defend you. Being well prepared will increase your self-confidence and enable you to be assertive about what's important to you.

Prepare and use good open questions

Prepare and use good questions to expose flaws in other people's arguments. Asking good questions is the most reliable way of gaining the initiative, and taking the wind out of someone's sails, in any situation. Questions that bullies dislike most are deep, constructive, incisive and probing, especially if the question exposes a lack of thought, preparation, consideration, consultation on their part. For example:

- 'What is your evidence (for what you have said or claimed)?'

- 'Who have you consulted about this?'
- 'How did you go about looking for alternative solutions?'
- 'How have you measured (whatever you say is a problem)?'
- 'How will you measure the true effectiveness of your solution if you implement it?'
- 'What can you say about different solutions that have worked in other situations?'

And don't be fobbed off. Stick to your guns. If the question is avoided or ignored return to it, or re-phrase it (which you can prepare as well).

Re-condition and practice your own new reactions to aggression: Re-conditioning your own reaction to dominant people, particularly building your own 'triggered reactions', giving yourself 'thinking time' to prevent yourself being bulldozed, and 'making like a brick wall' in the face of someone else's attempt to dominate you without justification. Try visualizing yourself behaving in a firmer manner, saying firmer things, asking firm clear, probing questions, and presenting well-prepared facts and evidence. Practice in your mind saying 'Hold on a minute – I need to consider what you have just said.' Also practice saying 'I'm not sure about that. It's too important to make a snap decision now.' Also 'I can't agree to that at such short notice. Tell me when you really need to know, and I'll get back to you.' There are other ways to help resist bulldozing and bullying. Practice and condition new reactions in yourself to resist, rather than cave in, for fear that someone might shout at you or have a tantrum. If you are worried about your response to being shouted at then practice being shouted at until you realise it really doesn't hurt – it just makes the person doing the shouting look daft. Practice with your most scary friend shouting right in your face for you to 'do as you are told', time after time, and in between each time say calmly (and believe it because it's true) 'You don't frighten me.' Practice it until you can control your response to being shouted at.

Have faith on your own abilities: Non-assertive people have different styles and methods compared to dominant, aggressive people and bullies. Non-assertive people are often extremely strong in areas of process, detail, dependability, reliability, finishing things (that others have started), checking, monitoring, communicating, interpreting and understanding, and working cooperatively with others. These capabilities all have the potential to undo a bully who has no proper justification. Find out what your strengths and style are and use them to defend and support your position. The biggest tantrum is no match for a well organised defence.

CHAPTER THREE

Body Language Basics

Leadership is about inspiring and empowering those around you to do better than they thought possible. Some are born to lead while others perfect it through practice and experience. Some leaders command respect the moment they walk into a room while others spearhead an entire group with their magnetic gaze and voice. So, what is it that makes these leaders such powerful, all-consuming forces to reckon with? Impeccable body language is a major attribute, of course. Posture, gestures, mannerisms, facial expressions, eye contact and the way an individual uses his/her personal space play a great role in making an impact as a leader. Here are the crucial non-verbal behaviors that HI Counselor has put together for every leader who wishes to improve his/her body language and shift those leadership skills to top gear.

Successful leaders use nonverbal cues — such as smiling and posture — to their advantage. Your nonverbal signals transmit a message to the people you are communicating with, whether in a one-on-one meeting or when you speak to groups. If you want people to trust and respect you, it's important to be conscious of what your body language is saying. Having the right balance of power and authority with warmth and empathy is essential. If your body language conveys too much warmth, it may limit your ability to command other people's attention. On the other hand, if you use too many power signals, you may appear cold and detached. Being mindful of your body language is important for two reasons. First, it can help you express to others that you are trustworthy and that you should be listened to. However, there is a second benefit to leveraging the power of your physiology: It can transform how you see yourself.

Decide what you want to convey: Almost everything we do – how we walk, talk, gesture, look at people, shake hands, sit down, arrange our office, dress, wear our hair, etc. – communicates something about who we are. So the first crucial step for leaders to consider is: Who is the 'I' that I present to my peers and teams? Am I conveying the qualities that I want to convey? Think about how we communicate trustworthiness: Good eye contact, showing respect and trust of one's peers or team members, demonstrating support in conversation non-verbally. It matters literally if you lean forward or lean back in a chair – one conveys interest and involvement, one begins to imply distance. So how you physically comport yourself can make an enormous difference. In short, the mistake to avoid is adopting body language that is out of sync with behavior that defines the leader you want to be.

Stay authentic: There is no one-size-fits-all approach. Instead, match your non-verbal communication to both your audience and yourself. Communication is a social experience, so when working on your body language, consider whom you are speaking with and what you want to convey. For example, if you want to be authoritative, use expansive body language (think 'manspreading') and big gestures. If you want to be friendly and put others at ease, consider using subtler gestures and taking up less physical space. "At the same time, your non-verbal communication should feel comfortable to you. This is not to say you can't improve your non-verbal communication – you can and should practice new habits like physically leaning in, power posing, using matching hand gestures, etc. However, if you constantly pretend to be a loud, super-expressive extrovert when you're really a more reserved introvert (or vice versa), this can be bad for your well-being. It may also come across as unauthentic. So consider how to match your non-verbal behavior to your true self.

The Power Pose: The way you pose your entire body can project you as an effective leader. Here is how you can strike the power pose: Bring your shoulders up towards your ears. Turn them back and then lower them. Maintain your shoulders back, and keep your head straight in a standing posture. This pose will make you appear confident. Expanding your space and height is an effective non-verbal method of showing your authoritative power. Stand tall and claim your territory if you plan to lead the course of a meeting. Set your feet down on the floor and cross your legs while being seated. Take your elbows off your body and stretch your arms. Extending your body language can alter how people view your appearance. It can also affect the way you feel about yourself. Stand tall or sit straight, aligning the body's structure in a manner that expands and creates space. This gives you the appearance that you're more powerful regardless of your position within the organization. Be conscious that your feet may be too close while standing. This could make you appear uncertain or uneasy. It will look more confident and trustworthy if you broaden your stance, and then relax your knees.

Gestures: Make use of gestures to reflect your leadership. The use of hands to communicate is more convincing provided you are aware of the meaning of each gesture. Gentle, controlled movements between your shoulders and waist are a great way to enhance your presence as a leader. In order to convey warmth and confidence, turn your hands at a 45-degree angle with your palms up. This shows that you have nothing to hide. You can also show your authority by turning your hands to the side when you sign. It is a nonverbal indication to show that you are in control of the situation. It is extremely effective when you want to emphasize a point.

Open and closed body language: Managers can go too far on either side of the spectrum. They can be too open and eager with their body language, which often makes teams and employees uncomfortable. For instance, a power pose can make leaders more confident presenters, but in certain circumstances (such as when you're the most influential person in the room), it can be seen as arrogance. "Or they can be too closed off, which will lead team members to believe their manager doesn't care. Leaders who keep their head down are often assumed to be meek or doubtful, so any decision they make would make the team feel unsure. The right thing to do here is to be relaxed and conscious of what message you're sending with your body language.

Listening: It's important for executives to convey to co-workers that they are in the moment and listening. Simple things help: Sit up, keep eye contact, use open movements while gesturing, and keep your fingertips lightly touching while resting your hands. Listening, relating, connecting emotionally – these are the values to express with your non-verbal communication. I would stay away from any gesture or movement that contradicts these values, such as crossed arms or slouchy spinal alignment.

Eye contact: Eye contact is incredibly important as a leader. Looking your team members directly in the eye and listening to hear (not just to answer) builds trust between a leader and their team members. When a leader is looking around and not focusing on the team, the leader seems distracted or insincere

Limit distractions: Pay attention to the person you are speaking with. It sounds basic, but with our many distractions (phone, text messages, tones that are coming from our computer or phones, etc.), we have never been more distracted as a culture. Your tone of voice is also something to pay attention to. Are you speaking with a confident, authoritative tone, or are you saying 'um' and hesitating with the words you are using? These will all be cues to the person you are interacting with.

Mirroring in one-on-one interactions: It's less about what you do and more about being cognizant. Just like you might pick the right keywords for a big speech, it's important to be as intentional about your body language, especially for sensitive or critical presentations, one-on-one meetings, etc. Consider mirroring. Next time you are talking to someone one-on-one, notice if they slant their head, if they speak quickly or slowly, how close or far they are from you, their posture, etc., and if possible, see if you can slowly replicate it. Do this only if you feel comfortable and it's not ridiculous. You will find that the other side feels more comfortable with you. It's the equivalent of them asking where you are from and you saying the same state – a nice ice-breaker and connection point.

Evaluate your own body language

For leaders who want to start working on improving their own body language, Towne has some actionable advice: "Use the next week you are in the office to ask yourself these questions each day."

Eye contact: "Are your eyes mostly on your laptop when you are in a meeting? Or looking down at your phone as you walk through the hallways or stand in the elevator? Who are the last three people you saw in the elevator or in the kitchen today? (Can't remember? You probably weren't looking at them – what does that convey?) Which people are you comfortable making eye contact with? Why? Why not with others?"

Body Language: "What are the first things you do when you enter a meeting? Open your laptop? Open a notebook? Wait for others to arrive? Play with your phone? Where are your hands during a meeting? When you speak, what are your hands doing? What is your relaxed hand position? What is your stressed hand position? Are you leaning forward or back? What is your listening posture? Arms crossed or down? How do you move your head during conversations? When you leave meetings to walk back to your office or to your next gathering, are you walking fast or slow? Is your phone in your hand or pocket/purse/bag?" Write down your answers and after five days, you will have solid data on how your body language is helping or hindering you.

The hand gestures you need to avoid as a leader:

Hidden hands: Try not to keep your hands out of sight as it tends to convey you are not trustworthy. Since ancient times, approaching someone without showing the hands signals potential danger and this symbolism is deeply ingrained in our minds.

Finger-pointing: It is impolite to point fingers at anyone. Many corporate executives, however, do use this gesture in meetings to show dominance. However, it is perceived by many as not an act of dominance but as a gesture of losing control over oneself.

Over-Enthusiastic gestures: Using one's hands to emphasize what we speak is a sign of confidence and being comfortable with oneself. However, due to a rush of adrenaline or enthusiasm, some individuals go overboard with their hands and become hyper expressive by raising the hands above the shoulder, moving around too much and animating their facial expressions to an unnatural degree. This instantly gives off the vibes that you feel inferior about yourself.

Strike the Right Balance: Sometimes leaders need to instinctively know when they need to be open and enthusiastic with the way they present themselves without making their team feel uncomfortable. For example, a powerful pose can make leaders appear more confident while doing a presentation. However, under certain circumstances as to when you're the most powerful participant in the group, being too enthusiastic could be perceived as arrogance. So, make sure you understand when to exaggerate or tone down your body language to suit the audience.

Focus on the Speaker: Though many think leaders always do the talking, effective leaders also engage in a fair share of listening to what others have to say. Be attentive to the person you're communicating with. Lean in towards the person who is talking to you. Nod in affirmation and maintain healthy eye contact. Your voice tone is another thing to take note of. Are you speaking in an authoritative, confident tone or are you simply uttering a monotonous "um"? These are all signals to the person you're talking to and will project your personality as a leader.

Communication Strategies

A leader is someone who inspires positive, incremental change by empowering those around them to work toward common objectives. A leader's most powerful tool for doing so is communication. Effective communication is vital to gain trust, align efforts in the pursuit of goals, and inspire positive change. When communication is lacking, important information can be misinterpreted, causing relationships to suffer and, ultimately, creating barriers that hinder progress. If you're interested in enhancing your leadership capabilities, here are eight communication skills you need to be more effective in your role. Poor leadership communications do not only result in a loss of customers but play a significant role in every other major area of a company's success including their ability to contend with competitors, keep employee retention low, and maintain adequate turnover.

It's critical. Good communication is a core leadership function and a key characteristic of a good leader. Effective communication and effective leadership are closely intertwined. As a leader, you need to be a skilled communicator in countless relationships at the organizational level, in communities and groups, and sometimes on a global scale in order to achieve results through others. You need to think with clarity, express ideas, and share information with a multitude of audiences. You must learn to handle the rapid flows of information within the organization, and among customers, partners, employees, and other stakeholders and influencers. Leaders must be purposeful and intentional about effective communication. You must know how and when to communicate, and select the appropriate mode for your audience. In fact, there are 4 types of communication contexts, including writing, conversing, presenting, and facilitating — and leaders must excel in all of them. It's the only way to meet people's individual needs and enable important human connections.

Effective communication strategies: For any leader aiming to improve their communications, there are a number of beneficial strategies that can help achieve this goal. Having well-thought-out plans in place is the most effective way for leaders to succeed in their overall objective of communicating clearly with employees, shareholders, and customers.

Clever leaders know that strong employee communications not only influence every aspect of a person's working life, they also contribute to a healthier financial bottom line. Engaged employees have a positive impact on a company, and effective internal communications are key to achieving this. A cohesive, direct, and targeted communications strategy will encourage workers to recommend the employer's products and services, solve emerging customer needs, and to be more innovative and productive.

A competent leader will understand the vital role employee engagement plays in driving employee productivity and business success. Poor communication is one of the biggest causes of low employee engagement as it leads workers to question what role they play in the company, how their superiors view their performance, and where the company is headed. Valuable conversations are essential to building trust, compassion, and clarity, all of which contribute to healthy relationships in the workplace. By establishing good internal communications, leaders will be able to keep employees informed, motivated, and engaged.

Receiving and Implementing Feedback: Asking for feedback from your team can not only help you grow as a leader, but build trust among your colleagues. It's critical, though, that you don't just listen to the feedback. You also need to act on it. If you continue to receive feedback from your team, but don't implement any changes, they're going to lose faith in your ability to follow through. It's likely there will be comments you can't immediately act on—be transparent about that. By letting your employees know they were heard and then apprising them of any progress you can, or do, make, they'll feel as though you value their perspective and are serious about improving.

Important Facts

Be honest and sincere. Find your own voice; quit using corporate-speak or sounding like someone you're not. Let who you are, where you come from, and what you value come through in your communication. People want, respect, and will follow authentic leadership. So forget about eloquence — worry about being real. Don't disguise who you are. People will never willingly follow someone they feel is inauthentic.

If you want to communicate well, don't be out of sight. Don't be known only by your emails and official missives. Be present, visible, and available. Getting "out there" — consistently and predictably — lets others know what kind of leader you are. People need to see and feel who you are to feel connected to the work you want them to do. Find ways to interact with all of your stakeholder groups, even (and especially!) if communicating in a crisis.

Good communicators are also good listeners. When you listen well, you gain a clear understanding of another's perspective and knowledge. Listening fosters trust, respect, openness, and alignment. Active listening is a key part of coaching others. Allow people to air their concerns. Ask powerful questions that open the door to what people really think and feel. And pay close, respectful attention to what is said — and what's left unsaid.

When a leader focuses on their contribution to the conversation, not just receiving their team's deliverables, they learn more and help the team get closer to accomplishing shared goals. A skilled leader and effective communicator is not only good at transferring their own ideas, but also excels in aligning expectations, inspiring action, and spreading vision. Sometimes focusing on the "leave-behinds" is just as crucial as focusing on the "take-aways."

CONVERSATION VERSUS COMMUNICATION: The communications cascade may seem like a hierarchical structured template for one-way communications from you to an audience. It does not have to be so. You may have positions and viewpoints you communicate through conversations and dialogue with other stakeholders. Indeed you may modify your positions and viewpoints based on the dialogues with stakeholders. Conversations are part of the communications process, useful for establishing mutual understanding and revising priorities and messages. The cascade, while appearing linear, is not meant to be a one-time effort. Instead it should be a dynamic process with feedback that is reviewed and reshaped every six months or so to be relevant, timely, and effective.

Align communications to your priorities. A good starting point would be your core go-forward priorities. In a previous article we looked at how to elevator pitch your top priorities. Once you have clarity on key priorities, it makes sense to create a communications strategy specific to each priority, which then becomes part of an overall communications program.

Define critical audiences. For each priority, define your critical audiences. Who do you need to communicate to? Who do you need to hear from? As an incoming Financial Head, for example, you can have many different audiences you need to communicate to. These may be your direct-report leadership team, your entire finance organization, the executive committee, the whole company. The first step to a communications strategy for a specific priority is to define the audiences.

Define audience-specific objectives around each priority. Let us assume that as a Financial Head, your priority is to create a more accountable finance organization that delivers insights and value to the businesses. With each audience, you are likely to have different goals. For example, initially, with your direct leadership team, your goal may be to have them step up and take more responsibility for decisions and delivery of insights to stakeholders. With the CEO and peer executives, your goal may be to demonstrate progress on your objective. Thus, for each priority you may have different communication intents and goals for different audiences.

Define critical messages. For each audience under a priority, there will be different messages at different points of time. From the above example of creating a more accountable finance organization that delivers insights and value to the business units, you are likely to have different messages for your staff and your business peers at different times. With your team, you may first want to communicate revised expectations. Next, you may want to communicate examples of behaviors and actions that create the value you want to demonstrate to the businesses. Finally, you may want to establish a scorecard that helps your team track progress against the objective. With your peers and the CEO, you may want to communicate timelines for forthcoming actions, such as upgrading select staff, and also report tangible ways finance added insights to the business to demonstrate progress on this objective. In short, having your straw man messages to different audiences clarified across a timeline can help with the effective construction and distribution of messages as needed.

Package your messages. Once you have defined some key messages, the next step is to consider how they are best packaged for delivery. The key here is that your intended audience understands and, ideally, responds to your message in a way that you want. So, will your messages be communicated as stories or will they be communicated in a factual report or data dashboard? Will the messages be communicated through direct requests and conversations? Different types of messages are best packaged in a format that best conveys the message. Generally where behavioral or belief changes are required, stories may be a more memorable and effective format.

Think through who will deliver the messages. When you define a communications program, you do not have to deliver it all by yourself. Sometimes it is more effective when others deliver messages on your behalf. Whether it is your leadership team or staff sharing their experiences in a town hall, including others in the communication of the message can help demonstrate critical team behaviors. When others deliver the messages in addition to you, it can show visible commitment from team and peer leaders. Peer stories may also be more powerful in their impact than top down messages.

Select channels for communication. Today, executives have numerous channels for communication within the organization and externally. Email, work networking systems like Yammer, LinkedIn, and Twitter combined with video, teleconferencing, and webcasting provide a plethora of electronic options with a wide reach. These can also be combined with in-person town halls and other meeting formats to combine in-person conversations and broad online communications. Select your communication channels depending on the nature of the messages, the importance of different stakeholders, the number of stakeholders to communicate to, and their geographic dispersion.

Define communication frequency. For each priority, audience, message, and channel, define the frequency of your communications. For example, as a Financial Head, you may work with the CEO and go over quarterly earnings in a companywide town hall. For your entire organization you may similarly do a town hall once or twice a year to ensure alignment of objectives and priorities. For other communications you may need to set up in-person meetings. Defining the frequency and channels can help clarify the demands of a communications program on your available time.

Seek feedback and evaluate your communications. To assess if your communications strategy is working, you may want to get feedback from your different audiences. You can get feedback from direct conversations with a sampling of your audiences, where you get a chance to assess how well they understand your messages and agenda. For events such as web seminars and town halls, you can use online surveys to gather feedback on the effectiveness of these communications. Feedback can help shape improvements to the communications program. The communications cascade above provides a systematic approach toward building a communications program. You can use it to ask an insourced or outsourced communications professional to shape a communications strategy for each of your individual priorities and audiences, and an overall program for you early in your transition. Given that attention is a scarce resource, it is important for the communications professional to design an overall program that is respectful of the different audiences' and your time. A good communications program also helps you assess how much effort and time you will have to put into communications. It will clarify your messages and ways of engaging critical stakeholders. An authentic and credible communications program can help persuade and inform key stakeholders on your intentions and successes, and this in turn can accelerate your impact on the organization

BEWARE OF THE INAUTHENTIC AND INANE: Today there is a proliferation of electronic communications channels within and across organizations—LinkedIn, Twitter, Facebook, and so on. As a leader, you may be counseled to be present on these channels by your marketing and communications staff; they may even write messages for you to disperse on these channels. Some even directly send messages on your behalf. Do not feel compelled to post communications on these channels just because they are available—doing so without care makes you look inauthentic and inane. For example, I often get recommendations on so-called thought leadership pop up on my LinkedIn feed from executives—with a one liner such as "Great article on the future of X industry." When you open the article and find it to be lame, it simply makes you think the executive who endorsed it is inauthentic or inane. They probably never read it (thus inauthentic) and probably left it to someone else to formulate their post. These new online channels are useful tools when you are authentic and credible in using them to effectively connect with key stakeholders. But beware of serial endorsing and other such online communication behaviors. Your name may appear frequently online but also adversely undermine your credibility. If you endorse a piece, say why it personally resonated with you and at least read it before endorsing it. Be discerning in your online communications and choose to be credible and authentic by truly personalizing them.

All too often, senior executives underestimate the communications effort required to influence and make a difference in their organization. Frequently, internal communications support for senior executives is either unavailable beyond the CEO's office or, when available, is ad hoc and not systematic. Working through the communications cascade early in the transition with a good communications professional can help you clarify your asks of them, and both frame and execute a systematic communications agenda efficiently to achieve your organizational objectives.

CHAPTER FIVE

Creative Problem Solving

The leadership skills they possess can significantly affect the quality of the innovative outcome. Consequently, as organizations increasingly depend on new products and processes to fuel their future, creative problem-solving stands as a critical leadership skill. For leaders, the creative thought process is sequentially different than for individual contributors. Specifically, successful leaders initiate the process by soliciting and evaluating others' ideas for solving a particular problem. The clearer the problem to be solved, the easier for team members to produce potential solutions and a leader to evaluate the quality of those solutions. Seeing and clarifying problems, either solo or in collaboration thus becomes the first challenge to a leader's creative skillset.

The second progressive task is **identifying potential solutions** to be analyzed and evaluated. Evaluating proposed solutions normally ignites the leader's creative thinking and they begin to generate additional ideas, discover alternative perspectives, and redefine the original problem. Sharing their alternatives, insights, and additions stimulates team members to continue solution generation and development. At this phase, solution standards are appraised, potential solution outcomes predicted, old ideas revised and new ideas put forth by leaders and contributors collectively. As potential and probable solutions surface, the third challenge for the leader becomes identifying and encouraging buy-in by the multiple stakeholders within the organization. As a result, the leader not only evaluates the potential logistical implications of solution implementation but also the social and political implications as well. Consequently, a leader needs to be skilled in evaluating creative ideas, as well as forecasting the varied outcomes associated with the different areas of the organization involved in the innovation.

A leader's creative problem-solving skills vary, however, depending on the type of problem being solved. Evaluative and judgment skills are in high demand if the problem requires a process innovation. When the solution is intended to result in a product innovation, a leader's skill in generating clear problem definitions and workable solutions will influence the ultimate success of the innovative outcome. For an organization to grow and prosper, fresh products and efficient processes are constantly needed. What worked yesterday is not guaranteed to work tomorrow. Leaders with creative problem-solving skills have the ability to stimulate, challenge and inspire others to continually pursue prominent problems and devise creative solutions to feed future organizational growth and success.

Steps an effective leader needs to follow to solve any problem

Identify the Problem: This is the first step to solving a problem. This may seem obvious; however, many leaders do not spend enough time defining problems, and as a result, they implement a solution prematurely. For you to truly define a problem, ask yourself, 'What is the problem?' and 'What should we be achieving instead?' The final question should be, 'How can I achieve this solution quickly and efficiently?' Once the issue is identified, you will be able to form an action plan for it with your team.

Evaluate the Problem: The next step prompts the leader to find the root cause of the problem. This is done by looking for overall patterns and asking questions about the what, who, where, when, and how to better understand the impact of the issue. Remember, this is not about assigning blame. Instead, leaders should evaluate and understand all the angles of the issue so that action can be taken moving forward.

Use Data to Back up Your Solution: Often, problems need to be explained to stakeholders along with a set of solutions if the problem is one that persists over time. By using data that you already have, you will be able to translate your discoveries into something tangible for others in your business.

Develop and Test Solutions: Once you have brainstormed a few solutions, you may want to start making those ideas actionable. You can do this by creating lists with accurate actions, timelines and prioritization. As a leader, you should be evaluating the cost and time for these results and communicating this info back to stakeholders.

Improve the Solution: Mistakes can only be evaluated from a hindsight perspective. Errors that occur should be part of a growth and development strategy. Leaders should use these mistakes to improve their overall approach, process and implementation plan. The most important thing about solutions is that they should be continuously improved upon over time.

Learn From Mistakes: Mistakes are a natural part of growth and development, and fostering solid problem-solving skills will likely entail some errors along the way. But mistakes can provide learning opportunities and improve your overall process and approach – as long as you appreciate them as a learning opportunity. Even if you aren't grappling with an obvious mistake, take time to reflect on the overall process and approach and determine if you would change anything to boost efficiency, creativity, or speed the next time. Cultivating strong problem-solving skills is critical for leaders at any level and career stage, and starting now ensures as you advance, you'll be fine-tuning this vital skill instead of trying to play catch up.

Communicate: You will need to cultivate good communication skills, to allow you to clearly and effectively relay the problem to key stakeholders. Then, you'll also need to inspire the people who are supporting the solution to remain connected to the task until it is resolved.Transparency is a key tenant of communication to ensure all aspects of a problem are understood. This is also critical when proposing solutions, as you need to understand different perspectives and concerns before implementing what you believe to be the right approach. Sometimes, this may entail keeping team members accountable for giving honest feedback, as not everyone feels comfortable sharing, particularly negative or dissenting opinions.

Focus on "Yes, And" Instead of "No, But": Using negative words like "no" discourages creative thinking. Instead, use positive language to build and maintain an environment that fosters the development of creative and innovative ideas.

Remove hierarchical silos: A problem is a problem. It does not know any hierarchical barriers. A great leader knows this fact. This is the reason they promote an open culture in the team. What does this open culture mean? Well, it simply means that there are no hierarchical barriers. A team member facing some problem could go ahead and seek assistance from their senior, without hesitating. Also, if he or she has a solution to the problem that any senior in the team is facing, they are free enough to go and share their views on how that can be solved. This is the first step in building trust within the team. A single person cannot have solution for all the problems. Great leaders embrace this fact. They know that they cannot do everything on their own. They value the capabilities of their team. They believe that success is a team effort, and not an individual one. By keeping the hierarchical barriers down, they actually give equal opportunities to everyone in the team to show their capabilities and become the future leaders – the problem solvers!

Developing strong problem-solving skills is a critical part of becoming a successful leader. Following these steps will help you boost your effectiveness, productivity, and catch any red flags before they hit.

CHAPTER SIX

Developing Creativity

Creative, innovative leaders have the ability to look at things in new ways and solve problems by seeing things others don't. Further, they build an environment that allows others to showcase their creativity and get outside of their comfort zone. By fostering a culture of innovation and ambition, teams are better equipped to problem-solve with innovative ideas, instill a competitive advantage, and remain dedicated to their mission.

Creative leadership will change the way organisations, people, and services are managed forever. Leadership and creativity work together to enable a dynamic workplace, innovative ideas, and elevated problem-solving that give organisations an edge over their competition. Oftentimes, creativity is overlooked in the conversation about the role of a leader.

What is Creativity?

Creativity is the use of imagination to conceive new ideas. When people hear the word "creativity" they often associate this term with artists, designers, and musicians. The truth is, creativity flows into every area of life, from relationships and communication to business strategies and organisational development.

Creative thinking is commonly used in business and is the process by which individuals generate new ideas or approaches to business, from building a strategy to inventing a product. Three primary types of creative thinking enable creative leadership, including:

- Lateral thinking: Involves breaking down existing processes and asking "why" at every stage to determine if a better method, product, or service could be developed.
- Deliberate creativity: Employs strategies and techniques to intentionally spur creative problem-solving, like approaching a problem from each person's perspective in an organisation to reach an equitable solution.

- Blue-sky thinking: Creating a safe space for brainstorming many possibilities and writing down many ideas without rejecting or dismissing out-of-the-box suggestions.

Creativity at Your Organization

The work environment matters: It is possible for companies to be more, or less, supportive of creativity. To foster innovation in yourself and your followers, the ideal company culture is one that values creativity. Leaders may want to give opportunities for employees to work together where possible[2], and reward employees for designing successful ideas or products. In addition, a creativity-supportive environment should acknowledge that not all ideas are successful ideas. That is to say, failure is an accceptable, and even necessary, part of the creative process. This gives employees the freedom, means, and encouragement to try new ideas. They can then approach problems in a new way without fearing punishment or retribution.

Leader creativity relates to follower creativity: In line with supporting creativity, when leaders model creative behavior to their employees, they are more likely to receive creativity in return. This may be due to a combination of other factors, such as trust, encouragement, and engagement. Where possible, try to apply new techniques or ideas in your work. This helps foster a supportive environment and shows direct reports that leaders value creativity. Once employee creativity begins, remember to applaud and reward new ideas to continue to encourage a more open environment.

Knowledge is key: One major aspect of creativity that is often overlooked is knowledge[2]. It follows that to create new ideas, products, or approaches, you need a thorough understanding. First, you must know the items that already exist. Further, you must understand how these items are flawed, and where to focus your attention. Finally, you must understand how ideas from one area can apply to another, making it easy to innovate by grouping many existing ideas into one new solution. Innovators don't pull ideas from thin air: they must understand the situation and the problem at hand. For organizations, this means ensuring your employees are well trained, and that they have access to ideas or procedures from other departments or companies that they can then apply to their own work.

Strategies for Growing as a Creative Leader

Creativity creates many enticing opportunities for both the leader and in the workplace. As a company expands, leaders spend more time on managing the business and can miss out on chances to be creative leaders and contributors to their team.

Use the following advice in your efforts to become a more creative leader in a busy, thriving workplace:

1. Keep educating yourself
2. Attend industry events
3. Rely on your team and foster teammate growth
4. Build thought leadership
5. Take time to be creative
6. Enjoy the creative process

These creative leadership approaches will ensure that you continue developing important leadership qualities in the workplace.

Continue to Educate Yourself: Continued learning is one of the most effective steps to take toward becoming a creative leader. Educational resources range from single articles to full-blown courses for individuals in leadership positions that teach strategies for creative leadership in the workplace. Leaders should also look to other individuals with experience when learning about leadership and management to take them to higher levels. Employees and other individuals in similar positions are fantastic resources for learning how to be a better and more creative leader.

Attend Industry Events: Events and seminars are a staple of corporate training and are employed by a great number of companies looking to advance team-building, leadership development, and management training. The same holds true when it comes to creative management training. Finding a seminar and attending it allows an individual a visceral, in-person resource for becoming a more creative leader.

Rely on the Team and Allow Them to Grow: A team can be an extension of its creative leader by providing their ideas and insights into day-to-day decision-making and problem-solving. Providing autonomy and some decision-making power to a team allows their creative leadership skills to thrive. Further, your employees will appreciate the creative freedom and trust you're giving them in the process. After all, 96% of engaged employees trust their management team. By relying on a team, a creative leader has more time and energy to focus on the bigger picture goals and ideas, which gives them the room to come up with new products or prototypes and new approaches. Giving your team room to grow on their own will benefit both them and you, the creative leader.

Develop Thought Leadership: Building a reputation as an expert goes a long way toward building trust as a creative leader. According to the Harvard Business Review's book Creative Confidence, communicating innovative ideas and documenting and sharing their evolution in search of new insights can communicate your thought processes to others. You naturally set yourself apart as an innovative thought leader in your field by providing creative leadership expertise.

Just a few recommended strategies for developing thought leadership in your industry include:

- Hosting webinars
- Speaking at industry events
- Joining industry roundtables
- Sharing insights on LinkedIn and other social media channels
- Creating content for your website
- Search out guest posting opportunities on other online publications

Each of these options gives you the chance to share knowledge and be an inspiration to others as a creative leader.

Take Scheduled Time to be Creative: Every creative leader needs time to clear their mind, reflect, and be creative. Creative leaders need to focus on big-picture ideas and reflect on what put them there in the first place: their creative vision. Most employees feel that they don't have much time in the day for creativity with their busy schedules. Companies like Google are known for creativity and note that some of their success in this arena comes from empowering their employees and encouraging expression at every opportunity. Quiet time exercising, being outdoors, meditating, and doing activities that quiet the mind can wipe the slate clean. In turn, this allows for time and clarity outside the busy day of running a company.

Have Fun: Having fun with your company team and industry peers creates an open, unstructured atmosphere that can spark creativity. Relaxing and enjoying activities with like-minded individual's leads to energized conversations and open-forum brainstorming. Communicating in an unstructured environment outside the workplace gets your mind off the daily grind and can lead to higher productivity with employees and peers. The creative vibe and energy that shines from a creative leader inspire the people around him or her.

Creativity is one of the most important characteristics of an effective leader and fosters a successful and healthy workplace environment. Creativity opens up opportunities for problem-solving, achieving goals, and inspiring teams to be creative and find unlikely perspectives.

Employing creative leadership-building strategies, such as continuing education, relying on trusted teammates, developing thought leadership, reflection, taking scheduled time out to develop creative skills, leaning on mentors, and just having fun with peers, are essential in the journey to becoming a successful creative leader in a thriving company. Companies looking to grow creative leadership on their teams may benefit from working with a top-ranked consulting team to get started.

Steps can help you be more creative at work:

Support creativity on a daily basis. There are a few things that you can do each day to help foster creativity in your department. First, develop your relationships with employees. A friendly, supportive relationship between leaders and followers is associated with greater creativity3. In addition, you can support innovation on a small scale. For example, leaders can hold problem solving meetings, where employees are free to share their ideas. This shows that your company values and desires critical thinking. Remember, most employees need to feel comfortable in the organization and with their leader before offering their own suggestions

Motivate to innovate. Research suggests that individuals who are more motivated in their job are more likely to be creative2. More specifically, those who feel autonomous in their job – that is, that they have control over how their work is done – are more likely to engage in creative thinking. Being successful at motivating oneself, as well as others, are key traits in a leader's toolkit, as motivated employees are generally more productive. Borrow lessons from your competency in Motivating Others and Achievement and Motivation to better help your employees to be creative.

Engage with the task at hand. For both leaders and followers, engaging in work relates to higher creativity. It may be that engaged employees have many of the other hallmarks that encourage creativity, such as a supportive environment, autonomy in their job, knowledge of their job, and the freedom to make mistakes. Perhaps engaged workers are more creative, or more creative employees are more engaged with their work. Either way, an increase in one is associated with an increase in the other. So, engaging in your work, or helping employees to engage in theirs, can positively impact innovation.

DR GAJANAN SHIRKE

CHAPTER SEVEN

Digital Citizenship

Things have changed, with a ton of advancements in technology, we now focus on developing digital leadership qualities and not just the age-old list of skills to imbibe. This has to start from a young age when the minds of the kids are fictile. Digital leadership is making use of technology, the internet, digital devices, and using it to benefit the status quo and transform outdated practices by collaborating and innovating. The whole concept of moving students from digital citizenship to digital leadership is to be understood in-depth. So, let's get into it.

Who are digital citizens?: As well as knowing what digital citizenship is, it's worth thinking about who the label might refer to. Again, we can turn to our open step for an explanation of this. A digital citizen is a person who develops the skills and knowledge to effectively use the internet and digital technologies. They're also people who use digital technologies and the internet in appropriate and responsible ways in order to engage and participate in society and politics. Effectively, anyone who uses modern digital technology can be considered a digital citizen. However, a *good* digital citizen is someone who is informed about the various issues that come with the incredible benefits of technology. This is why it's so essential to teach digital citizenship in schools and other educational institutions.

Why is digital citizenship important? : When we consider that essentially everyone with an internet connection is a digital citizen, the concept of digital citizenship becomes a critical part of our lives. No matter what age a person is, knowing how to stay safe, respect others, and participate meaningfully in our digital society becomes a necessity.

Because we are a global community: The latest statistics show that around 4.66 billion individuals worldwide are active internet users, roughly 65.6% of the world's entire population. As such, there is a global community of people, each navigating the digital world. With this incredible level of connectedness, we can communicate with people we may never meet, share content and stories to wide audiences, and access information, news, and media on demand. However, with this access comes potential risks.

Because there are risks that come with digital technology: The dangers of technology are numerous and varied. Whether its cyber security threats to our personal data, wealth, and identity or the dissemination of disinformation or illegal materials, the internet can be a dangerous place.

Because young people are increasingly online: Young people, in particular, face risks online. When you couple these stats with the fact that children spend over 20 hours a week online by the time they're in their teens, the need to understand and teach digital citizenship becomes apparent.

Digital Mission: The minds of the employees are usually very dynamic and creative. They come up with innovative ideas and solutions that sometimes are challenging to come up with even for adults. But they are also very volatile. Employees need to be taught to first vision their idea in execution and then develop a working mission towards the same. This will help them not deviate from their goal while surpassing set milestones. This mission should include how well they will utilize the digital resources given at hand to accelerate the run towards the achievement of their goal efficiently.

Practicing Advocacy: Now that the employees are encouraged and guided towards setting a mission for themselves, they should be led towards how to be advocates for what they believe to gauge the backing of the community. For this purpose, they can be taught how to rightly use social media platforms and school communication platforms, so they can set the tone for their projects and themselves as performers.

Community Collaboration: Advocacy will bring in support from the community and even peers, but how to collaborate with them to bring added value to their projects needs to be practiced. To evaluate who brings the most expertise required to outperform during the execution of the mission is something that will have to be taught and collaboration on several platforms like AI-based employees applications will prove to be beneficial, as it will give them insights in the efforts put and the results received.

Digital Entrepreneurs: You taught your employees how to effectively use technology and related aspects, they have even improved and enhanced their skills, but what next? Next comes teaching them how to be digital entrepreneurs. Basically, how to put all these learnings about and from technology, to develop a meaningful entity that they can take charge of.

Constant Upgrading: Once employees have developed the skills of a good digital leader, it is imperative to sustain and upgrade those skills. Learning never stops. Identifying new sources and concepts of learning and getting everyone to benefit from it displays digital leadership. This practice will also help these students when they start working as entrepreneurs or employees. Workforce collaboration by regular up-gradation of skills will get them closer to their ambition faster. The world and its demands are constantly changing, to keep up it is significant to enhance ourselves regularly.

Digital Leadership is more of an aspect of learning than its concept. To develop future leaders who are proficient within the digital world, garnering them from the early stages is the correct path to choose. Students will always be famished and capacious for learning new things, but the essentials of the learning modules are decided by the facilitators. So, teachers also need to realize the significance of these qualities and work towards inculcating them in their employees.

The elements of digital citizenship

Digital citizenship describes how we should act when using digital tools and interacting with others online to use technology in an appropriate, responsible, and empowered way. Before we get into the details of teaching digital citizenship, let's explore some of the key areas that need to be covered. Below, we've highlighted some of the essential elements of digital citizenship:

Equal access: Above, we mentioned that the COVID-19 pandemic has highlighted an issue around access to digital education. There are a couple of points to bear in mind with this issue. The first is to recognise that not all students have the same access to computers, smartphones, or the internet. Teachers and educators must be aware of this fact, ensuring that there are suitable alternatives that meet the needs of students. We cover the topic in more detail in our post on blended learning. It's also important to help students understand that learners, both their contemporaries and those around the world, may have different access to technology, either in the classroom or at home. There is a certain privilege and responsibility for those who do have access.

Digital skills: Those growing up in the digital age should be digitally fluent, able to use and understand the latest technology. Not only does this help them safely and securely navigate the digital world, but it also helps them understand how technology shapes our society. In our course on digital skills for work and life, learners can explore how our personal and professional lives are affected by the technology around us. This can act as a useful primer ahead of teaching your own students about digital citizenship. The current generation of learners will go on to shape the future of the digital world, so a thorough understanding of it can help ensure that everyone has a voice in what's to come.

Communicating online: We've already mentioned the issue of cyberbullying, but the aspect of online communication is broader than that. The vast majority of us communicate in the digital space somehow, whether through social media, instant messaging, or other formats. However, communicating online is often vastly different from in-person interactions. Nuance, tone of voice, body language, and other non-verbal cues aren't evident. What's more, the physical distance, relative anonymity, and lack of consequences mean that some people will act with less empathy. Working on emotional intelligence can help with self-awareness, self-management, social awareness, and relationship management, all of which can make us better at communicating in the digital space. We each have a responsibility for our actions online, and it's important to teach about the consequences of misconduct in a virtual space.

Data safety: One of the consequences of having our digital personas online is that we end up creating a digital footprint of our data. Whether it's creating social media posts, handing over personal details, or uploading our content to cloud storage, we each create vast amounts of data. As we explore in our post on how to protect your data, knowing about data safety can help you keep your rights and freedoms, prevent fraud and cybercrime, and ultimately, give you control over who uses your data and how.

Why and how to help employees improve their online presence

If your employees use digital technology at work, chances are they'll have an online presence. And by that, we mean any kind of information that can be found online and is attributed to them. Some of your employees (e.g., digital strategists, marketers, influencers, and active engagers with social media) will have carefully crafted their social media presence. But for most, their online presence will have evolved over time **without any real forethought or planning**. There's nothing wrong or unusual about this. But you can all benefit if employees improve their online presence. Developing a so-called "**professional online presence**" will help your employees better represent themselves *and* your company. And it isn't difficult. But most of your employees will require some training and structure to get it right. So, before you invest, let's take a look at the business case for that kind of training.

What benefits will helping them grow a professional online presence bring to the business? By encouraging them to network, and giving them the digital skills to do this more effectively, won't you run the risk of losing them? All fair questions. Which, if you're making a pitch for training, your stakeholders will want answered. So, here's the rationale:

Grow good digital citizens: With digital media comes responsibility or "digital citizenship". What is digital citizenship? Well, digital citizenship in the workplace is about giving employees in your organization the understanding and skills to **operate ethically in a digital world**. We should all think carefully about how we communicate online and the effect this might have on others. And encouraging your employees to conduct themselves with others in mind, and become good digital citizens, forms part of a wider duty of care package many employers are offering their teams.

Demonstrate standards: Employees who engage effectively and professionally online send out a powerful message about your business. They're living proof that your organization values and invests in technology, that you're forward-thinking and committed to developing high functioning cyber citizens. It shows that you trust and value your employees and know that they're confident and capable of representing your company in its best light. Because you don't just teach them how to use online channels, but also how to use them in the best possible way so they're **inclusive** and **respectful**.

Broaden your reach: By creating an online presence, your employees can network and meet customers and prospects wherever they are in the world. They can reach them in forums and communities where they spend their time and feel at home. Having a professional online presence also makes it easier for your employees to form new connections and grow your own business network. It makes your business more discoverable, too.

Do your research: Having a strong professional online presence means your employees are better-placed to learn about trends, industry developments, and industry influencers. And find out about what other companies (your competitors) are up to. A great form of research if you know where to look, it can help them learn about what customers want, their pain points, challenges, and wish lists.

Market your experts: If you've got employees who know their stuff, are good communicators, and confident in sharing their skills and knowledge, you're in luck. Help them grow their professional online presence so they can **share their expertise** with the wider world. Not only will their credibility and third-party recognition grow, yours will too.

Keep safe and secure: The more you help employees become informed and educated cyber citizens, the safer your business becomes. Data breaches and security threats are real risks to your business. Giving employees the skills to build an online presence that's safe and secure, reduces the risk of them disclosing sensitive information due to phishing or other cyber scams.

Show your face: Your people are your business. Investing in online presence management training for your employees means you can confidently share the human side of your organization.

Manage the personal vs. professional: How your employees interact digitally could reflect back on your organization. That's not to say that how they use social media for personal reasons needs to be monitored or restricted. They are, of course, entitled to their privacy. But how you, as an employer, can help them is by giving them the online presence management skills to separate their private and professional personas if they want to.

Improve not introduce: Digital media is all-consuming. And it's here to stay. Most—if not all—of your employees will already use social media and online networks on a regular basis. So, giving them the skills to do this more effectively is a simple and sensible way of recognizing this and making it work to your advantage.

Up skill your people: All training is good training. Offering employees training in online presence management demonstrates a commitment to their personal development and career progression—particularly if those skills aren't directly tied to their job. Yes, it could open up other career opportunities, but so will the acquisition of any new skills. And deciding to withhold training because you're afraid your employees will become more... employable (and possibly leave) just isn't an option.

Digital technology brings opportunities. Opportunities to connect and communicate—wherever and whenever. Opportunities to share information, content, and ideas. Opportunities for discovery, training, and education. And opportunities for business growth, profit, and career development. **But for every opportunity, there's also risk.** There's the risk it could pose to a business's brand or an employee's reputation. The risk around protecting customer data. And, where cyberbullying, fraud, and inappropriate and offensive content are concerned, a risk to an individual's physical safety and mental health. Employers who take digital citizenship seriously have the power to reduce those risks. In fact, they're the only ones who can really make a tangible difference.

CHAPTER EIGHT

Entrepreneurship

Someone who was motivating, collaborative, and kept the team moving toward a common goal. Perhaps this person had the authority of being a traditional leader, a boss or coach, for example. Or, it could be a peer who stepped up during an important project and thrived despite uncertainty and ambiguity. Chances are, part of what made this person so effective was that they were an **entrepreneurial leader.** When faced with the unknown, the best entrepreneurial leaders are good at experimenting, learning, and iterating. Compare this skillset to a more traditional "analyze, then act" leadership approach, and the difference is clear. A conventional leader might be great at assembling a puzzle when the picture is laid out to copy, while an entrepreneurial leader can dive in with no picture at all to start putting pieces together. Entrepreneurial leadership involves organizing and motivating a group of people to achieve a common objective through innovation, risk optimization, taking advantage of opportunities, and managing the dynamic organizational environment.

Many business owners take their leadership skills for granted. By default, they are the boss. Apart from their entrepreneurial skills and entrepreneurial mindset, doing business has all to do with people, so people skills and entrepreneurial leadership become eminent. With entrepreneurial leadership, two aspects come into play for the business owner: the kind of leadership style on the one hand and entrepreneurial skills on the other. A leadership style is viewed as a combination of different skills and behaviors that leaders use for interacting with their subordinates.

There are five leadership styles. **Leadership styles**

1. Transformational leadership: is all about attracting followers and considering their needs beyond the leader's immediate self-interests.

2. Transactional leadership: is based on the exchange of rewards for achieving results. Also called autocratic or authoritative leadership.
3. Culture-based leadership: leadership that focuses on common shared values, beliefs, ethics, and attitudes.
4. Charismatic leadership: motivates others to come up with innovation and creativity.
5. Visionary leadership: is based on painting that vision for the future and inspiring others to follow.

Besides entrepreneurship, leadership on its own involves a lot of fundamental skills – despite the type of leadership – that every entrepreneurial leader needs. Remember you don't need any degree or diploma to become a great leader.

Entrepreneurial leadership characteristics are as follows.

Communication skills: The leader is able to clearly articulate their ideas, and the plan to achieve common goals. They encourage communication between departments and across levels. They avoid ambiguities and generalizations, and are able to avoid conflict and misunderstanding due to poor communication.

Vision: A successful entrepreneurial leader has a clear vision. He knows exactly where he wants to go and how to get there. They communicate their vision to the team and work with them to make the vision a reality.

Integrity: There is no well-defined definition of integrity. A good reputation is a priceless business asset that can be earned only through consistently trustworthy behavior." followed by: "Integrity properly understood is not some add-on feature for business; it is at the core of sound business."

Active listening: Active listening is the ability to focus completely on the speaker and trying to understand their message. Note that active listening is not only directed to the entrepreneur. Active listening is also applicable to the employee. It's a two-way street, like in a partnership. An entrepreneurial leader encourages and ensures that both speaker and listener comprehend each others' message.

Supportive: An entrepreneurial leader realizes the importance of initiative and reactiveness, and they go out of their way to provide all the support that the team needs to achieve their goals. The leader usually does not punish employees when they take a calculated risk which misfires. Instead, they sit down with employees to analyze what went wrong and work with them to correct the mistakes.

Self-belief: The leader has tremendous belief in themselves and has confidence gained from years of experimenting, at times failing, and learning. They are aware of their strengths and weaknesses, and demonstrate their skills without hubris. An entrepreneurial leader is very self-assured.

Shares success: When the team or the organization succeeds at something, the leader does not hog the limelight or take all the credit. They acknowledge the contribution of others and shares the accolades with them.

Involved: You will not find an entrepreneurial leader cooped up in the office. Leaders like to spend time among employees, walk around the factory or department, interact with everyone, and see them doing their job. This leader will usually take some time out to informally chat with employees, and understand their work and personal challenges.

Create an atmosphere conducive to growth: With a deep understanding of the importance of other people's contribution to organizational success, the entrepreneurial leader creates an atmosphere that encourages everyone to share ideas, grow, and thrive. They actively seek other's opinions, and encourages them to come up with solutions to the problems that they face. The entrepreneurial leader also provides positive feedback when employees come forward with an opinion.

Vision: An entrepreneurial leader does business for a reason. An intensely felt mission gives them the drive to go and work hard for their company every day. What is it that they want to achieve with all stakeholders of their company? The vision is the concrete image of a point in time in the future, an attractive future picture of a beautiful reality where the lives of others have been improved.

Honesty: Honesty is the most important quality of an exceptional leader. Entrepreneurial leaders who are honest are able to quickly win the trust of their employees. People respect leaders to come across as honest, and are more likely to accept positive or negative feedback and also work harder.

Perseverance: When the going gets tough, the entrepreneurial leader perseveres. True entrepreneurs simply don't quit, they keep going till they find what they're looking for.

Learning: The leader not only invests significantly in learning and updating their knowledge, but they also create a learning environment in the organization encouraging others to improve their knowledge, widen their experience, and tackle multiple challenges. They encourage employees to think outside the box and come up with creative solutions to problems.

By developing and engaging these entrepreneurial leadership skills, business leaders can better influence their employees, foster trust and maximize the company's potential. When team members work toward common goals using an entrepreneurial approach to achieve business success, it can lead to exponential growth for companies. The ability to effectively lead is a crucial factor in the success, or lack thereof, in entrepreneurial businesses. By understanding and embodying what it takes to lead effectively, entrepreneurs can maximize their chances of success.

Key dimensions of entrepreneurial leadership.

Knowing yourself: Entrepreneurial leaders have a clear understanding of who they are and what is meaningful to them. They have a well-defined purpose in life and work. They are aware of their business purpose and a broad idea of how they wish to move forward. They understand how their businesses fit into their industry and their society. Those possessing entrepreneurial leadership qualities are also aware that they would need other like-minded people to form a great team in the absence of which the goals would remain a dream.

Focusing on the who before the what: A good leader focuses first on what to do but a great leader focuses on building the right team first. Like Jim Collins says in his book Good to Great, great entrepreneurial leaders make sure they have the right people on the bus and the right people in the key seats before deciding where to drive the bus. Building the right team is a battle half won and is a great leadership quality to possess. It is so important to find round pegs for the round holes so that the team is able to align with the common goal and move forward as one well-oiled machine.

Having a clear vision of the future: Successful entrepreneurial leadership demands that you have a clear vision of what you want to do and where you want to be in future. It is important to be able to think several steps ahead and not be limited by a short term view. Successful entrepreneurs never take the short cut. They prefer to have a clear long term vision well into the future and move towards that goal steadily. They are futuristic in their outlook and never suffer from short sightedness. They prefer to suffer in the short term but are seldom distracted from long term goals.

Great Communication Skills: Once the right people are in place, it is important to define the vision as clearly and concisely as possible. Clear articulation of vision is a common trait found in successful entrepreneurial leadership. The vision is clearly defined in his mind and well-articulated to his team so that they are aligned towards a shared goal. Both verbal and written communication skills are important for a great entrepreneur as it helps to express views clearly and inspire the team to share the vision and work towards it in a coordinated manner.

Adaptability: It is great to have a clear vision but it is also important to remember that we live in a dynamic business environment where disruptions can lead to paradigm shifts overnight. A key dimension of great entrepreneurial leadership is the ability to embrace this uncertainty and be ready to adapt to a changing world. It is this characteristic which helps them survive amidst disruptions by being able to think on their feet and adjust their vision to changed ground realities. You can take the example of Youtube or Facebook which have adapted well to changing business needs.

Continuous Learning: While research shows that more than 95% entrepreneurial leaders have a formal education, history is also filled with examples of geniuses like Bill Gates and Steve Jobs who left their education midway to pursue their entrepreneurial dreams. However, learning is a continuous process and never really stops for leaders who are always on the lookout for something new to learn. Especially in a fast changing world, replete with uncertainty and disruptions, no leader can afford to rest on past knowledge. It is imperative to keep in touch with the latest knowledge and industry developments, consumer behaviour, global events etc. It is also important to remember that all decisions may not be successful. It is important to learn from business failures as well and to convert them into learning opportunities.

Create an atmosphere conducive to growth: Entrepreneurial leaders, in general, possess a deep understanding of the vital role which other team members play in the success of the organisation. Such leaders create an atmosphere that encourages everyone to participate, share ideas, thrive and grow. They actively seek opinions from team members and encourage them to come up with creative solutions for the problems they face. They promote an environment of brainstorming and thinking outside the box which allows free exchange of ideas. The entrepreneurial leader also grooms his subordinates because he knows that he cannot do everything on his own and needs to groom the next line of executives.

We can safely say that the key dimensions of entrepreneurial leadership involves integrity of purpose, a keen sense of self belief, a clear vision, great people and communication skills, a flair for taking calculated risks, an ability to learn continuously and adapt to change whenever the situation demands. Go invent tomorrow instead of worrying about what happened yesterday. That's the essence of entrepreneurial leadership at its very best.

CHAPTER NINE

Interpersonal Skills

Interpersonal skills are often referred to as people skills, social skills, or social intelligence. They involve reading the signals that others send and interpreting them accurately in order to form effective responses. Individuals show their interpersonal skills all the time simply by interacting with others. Everyone has a personal style and an interpersonal style. Some people are more successful than others at using interpersonal skills for specific, desired results. Interpersonal skills may be based in part on personality and instinct. However, good ones can also be introduced to people and improved upon. While interpersonal skills can be developed, they cannot be learned solely from a textbook. For some people, they should be practiced, used daily, observed, and then tweaked. That is to say, these skills may come naturally to certain individuals, but others have to work at cultivating them. This cultivation often happens through continuous interaction with other individuals.

In many organizations, employees with strong interpersonal skills are valued for their pleasant demeanor and positive, solution-oriented attitude. These employees are seen as team players who work well with others to achieve a goal. In more human terms, everyone likes being around them. That's a welcome attribute in any social interaction, including those involving work. Interpersonal skills are strongly linked to a knowledge of social expectations and customs, whether that knowledge is inherent or learned. People with the strongest interpersonal skills adjust their tactics and communications as needed, depending on the reactions of others to their messages and meanings. Those without good interpersonal skills can still succeed in business if they are allowed to work in areas that don't require regular interactions with a variety of people. These areas might include research, development, coding, and system testing.

Improving Interpersonal Skills: Once acquired, interpersonal skills can be improved. They are best honed by practice. Expressing appreciation for team members and support staff, displaying empathy, moderating and resolving disputes quickly, and controlling displays of temper are all good activities for improving your interpersonal skills. Active listening can be practiced by repeating back a speaker's comment to make sure true communication is taking place. Furthermore, people can demonstrate their active listening skill by providing a carefully considered and appropriate answer. Courses often teach these skills and many firms offer them to their employees as a part of cultivating a strong workforce.

Types of interpersonal skills include being a good listener, understanding what's being said, and providing a positive, useful response. Someone with good interpersonal skills might decide to resolve an argument among colleagues that's preventing them from getting an important task done.

Interpersonal skills affect almost every area of business. Your people skills come into play when you enter into a negotiation, close a business deal or woo a client. They can help you build partnerships as well as a collaborative team environment. If you intend to be a leader and not just a manager, these are the interpersonal skills that you should hone:

Communication: Communication skills are a crucial interpersonal skill or trait that all effective leaders need to develop. Successful leaders need to be able to portray effective communication. Leaders with poor communication skills tend to veer into the command and control leadership style which is only effective in certain settings. Be specific with your directives and your expectations. Be clear and concise. Don't say in 1,000 words what you could say in 100 words. Also be careful with what you don't say. Nonverbal communication can convey just as much-if not more-than verbal communication. Your facial expressions, hand gestures, and body language can speak volumes during negotiations, interviews, trainings and team meetings.

Active Listening: Listen to understand, not to merely reply. Pay attention to each person you converse with and ask yourself what you can learn from that conversation. Let the members of your team know that you hear them. This will help them stay engaged and make them more willing to provide feedback when you request it.

Feedback: Feedback is essential for many reasons. The first and most obvious reason is that you want to maintain a consistently high level of performance from your staff. Being able to give constructive criticism is important in a leadership role. It is hugely valuable to you and the company to tell your employees what they are doing well along with what needs improvement. Over time, your team members will be more likely to appreciate your negative feedback if they know it is being presented with good intentions and while maintaining a positive attitude-showing, positivity, even in difficult situations, is key.

Trust and Honesty: Be as honest and transparent with your employees as possible, especially in times of crisis. Everyone will look to you for guidance, so it's up to you to give them reason to trust what you say and how you act. In the same token, display trust in your employees by not micro-managing them.

Selflessness: Your team is more likely to trust you and your leadership if they believe you have the best interests of the company at heart, and not the best interests of your own career. Show your employees that they are a priority and are valued members of the company through incentives and investments in their professional development. Plan one-on-one time with each member of your team; it shows that you value them and their contributions.

Self-Awareness: Be self-reflective about your own strengths and weaknesses so you can tap the right resources and do what's best for the company. You also need the ability to adjust your approach to the situation at hand. For example, if you are used to an autocratic approach but are now in charge of a team project, you'll need to acknowledge your usual style may not work. How can you adjust?

Set specific relationship-building goals: One of the biggest reasons to work on your interpersonal skills is to improve your relationships. If you have specific relationships in mind that you want to nurture, whether with a colleague or a boss, it's worth thinking about what about the relationship needs improvement and which interpersonal skills will help the dynamic. For example, if you and a coworker don't see eye to eye on a joint project you're working on, this is the perfect opportunity for you to work on your communication skills. Practice actively listening to your coworker to understand where they're coming from.

Compassion and Empathy: These two skills go hand-in-hand with self-awareness. With these skills, you can understand others' thoughts and feelings. When you are able to see a situation from another's perspective, you help to build trust and make people feel like humans and not just an employee ID

How to Improve Your Interpersonal Skills: Once you know where you stand, it's time to start planning out how to improve your interpersonal skills. Some of the best ways to improve are:

- Monitor your body language and ensure you're not doing things that make people think you're disengaged or aggressive (crossing your arms, looking around, avoiding eye contact, etc.)
- Practice active listening with family, friends, and coworkers – repeat what they've said back to them to ensure you're accurately listening
- Try being friendly and chatty with colleagues
- Practice leading a meeting or presentation
- Be enthusiastic and engaged when interacting with people
- Project an image of being confident and approachable

Technical Skills vs Soft Skills

When preparing a job application, the natural tendency is to focus on technical skills. It's only natural, as most job descriptions focus on specific requirements such as accounting, finance, Excel, financial modeling, and related skills.

key differences between technical and soft skills.

Technical Skills	Interpersonal Skills
IQ (Intelligence Quotient)	EQ (Emotional Quotient)
Following Rules	Changing Rules
Learned in School	Learned in Life
Easily Testable	Harder to Test
Can be Learned	Can be Learned
Heavy Focus in Careers	Equally Important, Less Focus

Enter Caption

Personal Branding

Personal branding is not just for Instagram influencers. Leaders can also benefit greatly by developing a personal brand that sets them apart. Do you have leadership potential? It's a loaded question that is raised often in performance reviews and promotion meetings worldwide. If you are beginning to think about advancing in your career, it is essential to understand how you are viewed in your organization and in your field. But other professionals – including your boss and your boss' boss – are increasingly pressed for time to the point where they generally cannot focus on recognizing or cultivating your skills; they're too busy putting out fires and worrying about revenues. If you want them to understand who you are and what you're truly capable of, you will have to make sure they take note.

A brand is a name, term, design, symbol, or any other feature that identifies one seller's good or service as distinct from those of other sellers." Creating such a brand, or "branding," is usually a deliberate and carefully crafted strategy. The process is designed to create a perception of what the product is, what it stands for, and what makes it special compared to other products on the market. Substitute the word "leader" for "product" and you have identified a new trend: the need for leaders to develop a personal brand. As with a product brand, a personal brand defines who a leader is and what differentiates him or her from others. Increasingly seen as a hallmark of good leadership, a personal brand can help to define and guide a leader's actions and contribute to his or her success. Developing a personal brand is not something to be done lightly. It is best undertaken with a solid knowledge of the traits that will generate results.

Personal branding: The first step, then, is being clear about the message you would like to send. Sometimes people conflate your personal brand with your "elevator pitch" – the short, pithy statement that describes who you are in 10 seconds. That is one element of your personal brand, but your brand is actually much more far- reaching: it is the totality of the message you send when people look at things like how you dress, how you speak, who you hang out with, what organizations you're a member of, what charities you support, whether and where you blog, the topics you talk about, and so on. That means your personal brand is not just something you tell people; it is something you live out every day, which is why authenticity is so crucial. Even if you wanted to, you can't sustain phoniness over time. Instead, the far better solution is to determine what is unique and powerful about who you are, and find ways to leverage that to your professional advantage. Start with a quick, informal poll of a few friends or colleagues: if you only had three words to describe me, what would they be? This forces people to focus and only list what they view as your most important characteristics. After you speak with three or four people, you'll begin to see patterns that can be quite illuminating. As executive coach Alisa Cohn told me when I interviewed her for Reinventing You, it's essential to compare the adjectives you hear with the ones that are necessary for where you want to go.

The process to developing a personal brand in five steps:

Identify Your Values. Who you are and how you treat others influences your ability to be an effective leader. What do you stand for and what will you not stand for? What do you want to be known for? What role did your values play in key successes or failures in your life? What values do you admire in others? Remember, your brand must be authentic, so do not attempt to adopt values you don't actually hold.

Understand Your Current Brand. You already have a personal brand — everyone does. You earned it automatically through your previous actions and behaviors. But your current brand may not be the one you want. Ditching your old brand starts with assessing how others perceive you. Ask for feedback from your manager, teammates and family regarding your communication and decision-making styles, strengths and weaknesses. Note common themes and areas for improvement.

Decide Where You Can Make a Difference. Your brand must encompass your unique contribution to an organization or project. Think about your current impact and the results you hope to deliver. Also consider who will benefit from your work, such as customers, investors, employees and the company. Focusing on this path will help you say no to distractions.

Craft Your Personal Mission Statement. A personal mission statement is a clear, purposeful promise to yourself, your work colleagues and your family. It answers the big questions your team may ask — who are you, what do you stand for, and how do you work? Craft your statement, then follow it.

Live You're Brand. Brilliant leaders are strong and consistent; poor leaders are tentative and unreliable. Build trust in your brand by living it every day. But do not assume your brand will stay the same forever — it won't. Take time to reflect, learn and evolve as your goals and circumstances change. Tweak your brand as necessary to shift with the times — and remain the best leader you can possibly be.

Know Your Personal Brand as a Leader: What are you known for as a leader? What do you represent? What do you stand for? To find your v-o-i-c-e as a leader is to live your Values, create your Outcomes, use your Influence, be Courageous and wrap it all up in your unique Expression. It is all about how you share your personal brand as a leader with your team, your peers and colleagues, your clients, and your community. Become a stellar communicator. Create followers. Contribute your talents and capabilities. Build and re-invent your personal brand so you remain renewed and refreshed. By taking that stand, voicing your opinion, making yourself known, communicating what matters to you...you are expressing who you are with your voice. You are expressing yourself as a leader.

Expressing yourself: is not just about you. It's about the relationships you foster with your clients, customers, colleagues, team, and your community. It's about the connections you make with people and the relevance of your message. It's about the way you carry yourself, your non-verbal language. It involves communicating the vision you've created for your organization and influencing and enrolling others to come along on your journey.

Expression: As important as good communication is, expression is more than just speaking, writing, and listening skills. Expression is establishing your personal style as a leader so people know in an instant what you stand for and how you'll react in a given situation. To sharpen your ability to express yourself.

Develop open and consistent channels of communication: One way to exercise courage is to listen more than you talk. That also applies to communicating your expression. When you listen, you get input and feedback from others that can help you perfect your brand, your project, and how you interact with others.

Instill confidence and inspire commitment: When you express your values, know your outcomes, have influence, and are courageous, people will naturally want to follow you as a leader. They will know who you are and what you represent. Being consistent and confident through a persuasive personal brand and presence is a key part of building your expression.

Spark curiosity and garner interest: What makes you tick? What are you passionate about? By being creative and sparking interest in your values and your vision, you encourage others to do the same and to help them gain confidence in their abilities of what they can accomplish.

Handle situations calmly without becoming emotional: We are human and can react to situations in a variety of ways. Anger, pre-judgment, and emotional outbursts can easily derail an otherwise strong leader. If you tend to be emotional, practice waiting until you are calm enough to address stressful situations.Know your trigger points. When you have confidence in your ability to handle confrontations calmly, they become less intimidating and people will actually look to you for your leadership when such a situation occurs. Don't express critical ideas when you are not emotionally centered and grounded.

Leadership skills for building a professional brand

At work and in life, how others perceive you is incredibly important. After all, others often define leadership – and the skills required to enact it. For example, you may believe you're trustworthy, but ultimately, it's up to those around you to form an opinion. The perception of others about you professionally is called your personal brand. A personal brand is a definable, largely uniform impression based on an individual's behaviours and achievements. The behaviours and achievements lead people to form opinions about an individual's experience, expertise and overall competence. Given that impressions are everything, the importance of leadership skills in building a personal brand can't be underestimated.

The best way to ensure your brand as a leader spreads throughout your organization is to make an effort to network. Not in the sense of going to "networking events" and trading business cards – instead, it is about breaking out of the ruts that we typically fall into as professionals. Most people eat lunch with the same people and talk with the same colleagues all the time. It is easy and comfortable, but it is also a mistake. Something as simple as inviting one new person in a different department out for lunch each week can have a dramatic impact on your ability to access best practices, connect with others, hear about opportunities and add value to your organization. Networking doesn't have to be an exhausting form of glad-handing; rather, it is about keeping yourself open to new encounters and new possibilities, and ensuring that you don't allow your connections to stagnate. If you want to keep your career moving forward, it is important to do the same with your network. Personal branding is a powerful way to distinguish yourself as a leader. When done right, it is the ultimate form of authenticity because it makes clear the value you can add and draws people to you, specifically. An investment in these strategies is one of the best forms of career insurance you can make.

CHAPTER ELEVEN

Project Management

A project leader is someone who leads a project, but that doesn't really get to the bottom of this seemingly simple title. There are project managers, who are responsible for many of the aspects that we associate with leadership. They assemble the team, devise the plan and manage resources to maintain the schedule and keep within budget. But leadership is a quality that should be expressed by everyone. It's not just leading by example, such as the project manager rolling up their sleeves and joining in on the work as needed, but everyone on the project team must take a leadership role. They need to own their responsibilities and manage the tasks assigned to them. The last thing anyone wants is a team of robots who can't make a move without being directed. That said, there is a project leader and their job is different than that of the team they manage. They have to straddle many worlds being both technically organizationally adept, able to engage effectively across boundaries, connecting talent with key challenges. Think of a project leader as the consummate integrator. They help others succeed.

Strengthen yourself as a Project Leader

A good place to start is with project leaders you respect, who have experience and have lead projects in ways that you wish to emulate. Seeking out help from a mentor is recommended, because they can add a depth of dimension to the process that all the books in the world can never touch. Another thing to do is keep in mind these six concepts that are like a leadership workout. Practice them and you'll strengthen your leadership muscles.

Mind the Gap: Take time to explore the gap between navigating and leveraging the tools of the trade and leading others. Its leadership in a classic sense, with the goal to bring to life a group of individuals that coalesce as a team and pursue high performance. Easy words, tough tasks, but worth the investment in time and attention.

Reframe you're Challenge: It's Not the Project, It's the Team: The issue you face isn't project execution, its team development. If you take care of the team and ensure that you form and frame the right environment, the team will take care of the initiative.

Let the Team Define Your Role: Perform a pre-post mortem on your role as leader. Ask your team: "At the end of this project when we are successful, what will you say that I did?" Listen carefully and you will hear many of the raw ingredients of high performance teams. From alignment on the purpose of the project to treating team members with respect to ensuring fair and even accountability to setting expectations high to not micro-managing, this question will prompt a torrent of important answers. Take notes. These define the raw content of your job description as project leader.

Teach Your Team How to Talk: In my many observations of teams struggling to perform, one of the common performance killers is an inability to navigate the swirl of emotions, biases, opinions and agendas that invade all of our group discussions. Spend time focusing on strengthening your facilitation skills.

Teach Your Teams How to Decide: Teams succeed or fail based on how they navigate moments of truth in the form of key, often irreversible decisions. And while strengthening your team's ability to talk as outlined above is important, supporting the development of effective decision-making processes is mission critical. Given the complexity of group decision-making, including our tendency to draw on our own unique prior experiences and to unknowingly impose our biases on a decision-choice, helping a group develop effective decision-making processes is no small task. You need a process. Look for the one that works for your organization and team.

Everyone Communicates, Leaders Connect: The people on your team are neither resources nor automatons. Great leaders at all levels strive to connect with team members on something a bit more personal than status meetings and reports. They take the time to engage and where appropriate, they strive to learn about the aspirations and even personal interests of their team members.

Roles and Responsibilities of a Project Manager: Project managers are responsible for building, maintaining, and managing projects. They decide which projects to work on, when to start and finish the project, who to hire, how to manage the project budget, and when to release the finished product.

The project manager, a primary point of contact for all stakeholders, manages the day-to-day operations of a project. Besides detecting and resolving issues to help solve problems that arise, some other key roles of the project manager include:

- Identifying the project goals and objectives
- Establishing the project scope
- Determining how much time to spend on each project
- Prioritizing the most important tasks
- Estimating the scope of work and the amount of resources required for it
- Evaluating strategies and improving them
- Ensuring that each developer has access to resources and tools needed by them
- Setting up deadlines for completing tasks
- Working with developers to write documentation and code reviews
- Developing and maintaining documentation for the software
- Managing project schedules, resources, and budget
- Conducting meetings and reviewing progress

Skills That Every Project Manager Needs

Project management skills are indispensable for successful project execution from beginning to end. Strengthening your project management skills is vital, as excellent project management skills can not only have a positive impact on your assignments, but they can also help you quickly climb up the career ladder. Here is a shortlist of the must-have project manager skills:

Communication: Project managers must have solid communication skills to convey messages and reports, deliver presentations, and share visions, ideas, and goals with all project stakeholders.

Negotiation: Successful project managers demonstrate excellent negotiation skills when dealing with customers, suppliers and other relevant parties. They also use their negotiation skills to manage conflicts and ensure that everyone achieves their project goals.

Risk Management: There are risks involved in every project. For this reason, project managers must have the expertise to implement risk mitigation strategies. They should have the ability to use enterprise-grade risk management tools that allow for effective analysis of potential risks.

Team Management: Project managers must be proficient team management professionals, with respect to the delegation of responsibilities, conflict resolution, performance evaluation, and motivating members to facilitate progress and improvements.

Budget Management: Creating viable project budgets is one of the key responsibilities of project managers. They need the right skills to generate spreadsheets, track costs throughout the project lifetime, and identify areas where costs are exceeding.

Problem-Solving: The ability to solve complex problems is a hallmark of every successful project manager. Expert project management professionals are quick to identify problems and offer systematic approaches to solve them.

Motivating and inspiring: Leaders develop a vision and then continually communicate that vision throughout the organization, working with the team to achieve the vision. Leaders keep their people enthusiastic in doing their work and focused on the project vision. They encourage the team members to do their best and accomplish the work with full self-satisfaction for the making their contribution towards the project vision.

Listening and influencing: Leaders are active listeners, understanding and considering the team members' perspective before making team decisions that will affect the team. Leaders get project team members and other stakeholders to collaborate and cooperate with each other, working towards a common goal.

Reporting: Project managers should be competent in preparing first-class project reports for evaluation. Reporting skills are essential for coordination with management, team members, and clients. This helps set clear goals, expectations, and outcomes.

Project management is different from leadership. Successful project managers may not be effective leaders. But project managers can develop leadership skills to become effective leaders. And organizations today need successful project managers to be effective leaders, as well. By understanding the difference between project management and leadership, and taking the path to become effective leaders, successful project managers can utilize their innovative and creative skills to help them develop leadership skills that will complement their project management abilities. The common aspect of project management and leadership is the yardstick by which the performance of both the project manager and the leader is measured. The performance of a project manager and the effectiveness of a leader are both measured in terms of the performance of the followers—the performance of the team. Hence, developing leadership skills for project managers with focus on skills to improve team performance should be an important consideration in leadership skills development for project managers. Essential leadership skills for project managers start with motivating and inspiring teams and individuals, and include negotiating and communicating skills, listening and influencing skills, and team building with emphasis on utilizing these skills to improve team performance.

CHAPTER TWELVE

Remote Effective Teamwork

Leaders are no longer resigned to just look for talent in their local geographic areas, workers from around the world can be considered due to advances in remote work technologies. Also, due to globalization, increase attention to the topic of work-life balance, and the advent of teleworking as an attractive perk, leaders increasingly have to manage remote work teams. If leaders thought communication was important before, remote groups have an even greater necessity for it. Managing contracts, software packages, work times, time zones, and company retreats and events are all factors leaders have to watch out for. Even though this can be a difficult task, there are a lot of advantages to managing a remote team.

Challenges of Managing Remote Work Teams

Costs of Technology: While leaders can save costs in rent and office space, workers also need software and technologies to get work done. This can be a sizeable amount of money depending on the type of work and what employees need to collaborate. There are low-cost options out there, but leaders need to make sure they purchase quality technology.

Handling Tech Issues: One benefit that employees who reside in in-office settings can enjoy is having easier access to IT teams in the event there is a tech problem. Having support teams handle tech request for employees in multiple time zones can be daunting and can slow down production.

Lack of Communication: Because most conversation will happen in written form whether, in an email or online collaboration software, leaders have to make sure their writing is clear and concise. This also goes for workers as well. This idea can be difficult to instill in someone who does not have experience with this skill. It is also likely that something in an email can be interpreted differently depending on who is reading it, so workers have to be sure they are ready to pick up the phone in case of a misunderstanding.

Aligning Schedules: What if a meeting is necessary? How can leaders ensure that everyone is able to be a part of the meeting if many of those on the remote team are in different time zones? This can be challenging to overcome. **In some way, someone will have to meet at a time that is not a part of their normal office hours.**

Lack of Social Interaction: Some workers benefit when they can have social ties and friendships with their co-workers. Working on a remote team makes this more difficult to do. Workers have to deal with isolation and a lack of communication that does not have to do with work tasks. This event can lead to stress and feelings of disengagement.

Selecting the Right People: Everyone is not cut out to work on a remote team. They may be a skilled employee who works well in an in-office environment, but they may not thrive as they work from home. Leaders have the challenging task during interviews of asking the right questions to weed out those who may not be right for remote work arrangements. Leaders may even have to let team members go if they cannot adjust.

How you can get remote teams to work together well:

Create a sense of normalcy: When the pandemic hit, millions of people's work routines changed. Some were furloughed and had to file for unemployment. Even the lucky ones worried about their job security and productivity at home. To support teams, we found small ways to make things seem "normal." Create a daily vlog to keep employees informed on company shifts and leadership decisions. Also let employees take whatever they needed from the office, delivered snack bags to remote employees. Even if your company doesn't have much to spend, it can still create normalcy through its traditions and processes.

Centralize your knowledge: When everyone is in the same office, it's easy to pop over a cubicle to ask a question. When you're working remotely, you need a one-stop shop for company knowledge. Tools like Slack make it easier to ask quick questions, and project management systems centralize work. Neither can take the place, however, of a corporate wiki or knowledge base. Your team needs at-a-glance access, not just to each other and their task list, but also to all of your company's key processes and documents. Creating a company encyclopedia takes time, of course. Encourage the leader of each team to brain-dump about its core responsibilities, initiatives, documents and histories. Appoint an editor to clean it all up, checking back once a month or quarter to update old entries.

Establish guidelines for face time: We tend to think about communication as words, but nonverbal communication is a crucial part of how we interact. When you're simply asking team members to complete a survey, a Slack message or email is enough. But if you're trying to get your marketing or sales teams buy in on a new campaign, hopping on the phone is a smart move.

Decide as a team: What circumstances call for a video call? Default to video when discussing:

- Any decision involving multiple teams
- A topic that's personal in nature, such as mental health issues
- Team-ide updates, such as a new HR policy
- Status changes, such as hirings, layoffs and furloughs
- Company culture events

Draw clear boundaries: Teams need clear expectations to work together effectively. Should people feel free to take a walk during the workday? If a remote team member gets sick, are they still expected to work that day? When they take lunch, should they set their status to "Away" in Slack? Particularly important while working remotely are work-life boundaries. Give workers clarity around what's OK and what's not. Perhaps hour-by-hour time-boxing doesn't make sense for your customer service team. Instead, you might ask them to choose one day each week to engage in deep work, such as adjusting their script. Get buy-in from your team on those boundaries. If someone has a suggestion around how time-boxing can be implemented, hear them out. Their idea might just work, and they'll respect you for taking their input into account.

Create a virtual water cooler: Whether workspaces have a literal watercooler, every organization has a metaphorical one: a space where they talk about everything from movies to politics to the new restaurant in town. Organizational psychologists attribute the "watercooler effect" to a 10% to 15% bump in productivity. Why would off-topic conversations help workers get more done? Because workers feel more connected to one another when they're able to communicate casually. Replicating this phenomenon virtually can be tough. Set up a channel in your instant messaging system where employees can unwind. Use small prompts to get them talking: What's their current favorite show on Netflix? Whose recipe is a must-try? Just as valuable are virtual happy hours. At the end of a tough week, put a Zoom call on the calendar with no purpose other than hanging out. For bonus points, have each employee's favorite drink delivered to their house.

Provide plenty of feedback: Like everyone else, employees are adjusting to the "new normal." They need to know that they're on the right track. Feedback, like water-cooler conversations, happens naturally in the office. But when everyone is remote, you have to be intentional about it. Give your team feedback formally and informally. Formalize it with periodic performance reviews, post-project commentary and peer surveys. Informally, you can:

- Provide in-the-moment pointers
- Pass on client compliments and criticisms
- Check in "just because" on Slack
- Reward wins with gifts, such as gift cards or delivered meals
- Ask how you can help when someone seems stressed

As a leader, supporting your team should be a top priority. Make sure your staff knows their hard work doesn't go unnoticed.

CHAPTER THIRTEEN

The Cloud and Business

Cloud computing is one such tech trend that has gained excellent momentum in the recent past in business leadership. Yes, cloud technology that was once perceived by tech pundits as a marketing gimmick has evolved into a promising and apparent vision for new age computing. The unparalleled potential of cloud computing to boost business performance has led businesses embrace it on a wide scale. Cloud computing by offering unparalleled mobility for employees and scalability for businesses is transforming the way organisations do business. This is why business leaders of today's era ought to be well-versed with technological advancements and their application.

When it comes to data storage, processing and collaboration, many businesses choose the flexibility and convenience of cloud computing over traditional local hosting and on-premise software. With cloud computing, you can access and store data and applications online instead of on a hard drive. If your company uses Google Docs for editing and document collaboration, Dropbox or Google Drive for file storage, Slack for cross-team communications, or online CRM software for managing sales, you're using cloud computing. Working in the cloud offers small businesses many benefits, including enhanced collaboration, easy access and fast turnaround. However, cloud computing drawbacks include security concerns and fewer customization options. We'll explore cloud computing, how it works, cloud services to consider, and the pros and cons of cloud computing for small businesses.

Cloud computing: Cloud computing is the on-demand delivery of computing services, including applications, data storage and data processing, over the internet. You'll usually pay for cloud computing services on a pay-as-you-go basis, so you pay only for the applications and cloud services you use. This approach helps lower your business's operating costs and allows for flexible scaling. In today's ever-changing business climate, small business owners must be able to access data and applications from their computers, tablets or mobile phones whether they're in the office, out in the field or on the road. Cloud computing provides this anywhere access via an internet connection.

Business Scalability: Because of the market's uncertainty, companies have traditionally struggled with scaling. The scalability of cloud computing allows companies to grow effectively. As the company expands, companies may increase their infrastructure and facilities without having to predict server needs or purchase additional storage capacity. All you have to do now is contact the service provider to modify your subscriptions. To increase operating efficiency, the provider will then allocate extra space based on your specific needs. When a firm is rapidly expanding, it is simple to scale up its services utilizing the cloud infrastructure. Likewise, anyone who desires to reduce the criteria can do so without difficulty. Another key commercial advantage of cloud computing is that leading IT companies across the world appreciate is operational flexibility. Cloud computing has improved throughout time to effectively assist organizations that make use of this transformative technology. Businesses need the means to enhance their efficiency, productivity, and overall performance in today's modern competitive climate, and cloud technology offers a flexible means of expansion.

Cloud Contributes to Digital Transformation: Today, a large number of organizations are undergoing digital transformation. Admittedly, it's one of the most effective methods for businesses to stay competitive in today's modern congested market. Nonetheless, becoming paperless is only one aspect of digital evolution. Digital transformation entails a comprehensive technological change of corporate processes. This means that businesses will move their whole operations to the cloud. Many businesses are still unwilling to make this change. The major reason for this is because it is an expensive and sometimes complicated operation to integrate existing data centers into the cloud. Nobody likes delays for migration, and no one wants to risk a bad migration that costs them a lot of money. Thankfully, such businesses may effectively outsource the entire relocation process. In reality, you can discover reputable firms that will assure appropriate cloud implementation. This way, you'll be able to make a painless and seamless transfer to the cloud. Every firm will have to contemplate a digitalization eventually as old methods of operation become increasingly expensive and outdated.

Secure Collaboration: Business technology, like other new software, is updated on a regular basis for security updates, additional features, and bug fixes. Because cloud technology leaves the obligation for updates on the cloud software provider, technical assistance can be more effective. Consequently, the need for businesses to develop and sustain a complete IT workforce responsible for communications infrastructure, security updates, operating software updates, and staffing customer help centers are practices that are quickly becoming obsolete in the wake of the more agile option of working with IT service providers. Many organizations rely on connectivity, and cloud computing can provide quick, simple, and trustworthy communication for members of the team all around the world. Any team member may retrieve data in the cloud at any moment for inspection, changes, or comments. A virtual employee may contribute to the work or project and share his idea with other team members. Additionally, Cloud can be the best possible solution for collaborating with two or more teams. For example, an app-based company is using the cloud. Then, all the UI/UX designers, architects, engineers, digital marketing team, and product managers can collaborate and communicate easily with each other. They can check each other's work efficiency and their performance.

Easy Access: Cloud computing also allows for quick data access, processes, and critical business applications from any place with a reliable Internet connection across the world. Businesses no longer need to bring a tablet or laptop with a comprehensive set of business software and specialized apps. Alternatively, customers may use any browser-enabled device. Experts can get back to us as soon as they obtain a new computer if one malfunction or is taken. As the software is stored on the cloud, there is no need to worry about updating or activating it if it is lost or stolen. Encryption key data in cloud storage is no exception.

Easy Data Backup and Recovery: One of the most significant advantages of cloud computing is storage space. Any company data that is relevant may be kept on the cloud, allowing connectivity and usefulness. Your data, on the other hand, can be accessed from every platform and from any location on the globe, making it perfect for remote employees and businesses.

Furthermore, the cloud includes a built-in data backup and restore system that ensures your company's data is fully protected. Your information is safeguarded against computer hackers, natural calamities, and even outright unauthorized access. Your information is never kept in a single location, which is how it works. Instead, it's broken down into pieces, encoded, and dispersed across many locations, such as faraway cloud services. Even if a computer hacker stole your information from a single site, it would be fragmented and useless. You also have backup data saved in the cloud, this implies data can be retrieved quickly and your firm may restart activities as if the tragedy never occurred.

Cost Efficiency: As previously said, a cloud computing platform allows businesses to access services on a need-basis. Consequently, the cost-effectiveness of cloud computing is one of its main advantages, a game-changer in the corporate world. Cloud computing is a subscription approach, thus there are no upfront expenses for hardware, software, or maintenance. Only the services you're now utilizing have monthly membership costs. You may easily cease paying for services when you no longer have the need. Applications, systems, infrastructures, and other IT requirements are all included in cloud services.

Enhanced Customer Service: Employees may now receive data that will assist them in serving consumers at any time and from any location. They may interact with possible consumers through the cloud using a variety of devices, including mobile, laptop, and desktop computers. Customers require high-bandwidth information, such as how-to videos. Larger companies aren't the only ones with this ability. Small businesses can also benefit from cloud technologies to deliver wide throughput. A self-service website is increasingly commonplace in many businesses. Customer issues may be resolved quickly and effectively as a result. Thanks to the use of cloud, the service desk is streamlined with increased automation. This enhances overall customer satisfaction by reducing ticket times and quickening issue responsiveness. Concerns received across different channels may be handled using the cloud's omnichannel assistance. This allows for more transparency and better monitoring of ticket submissions.

Improved Innovation: The use of cloud services can help to create a workplace conducive to innovation. Once the operational and technical elements are in the right position, companies can redirect and redirect their attention to the advancement of transformation initiatives. While server management has no impact on organizational performance, data management improves quality and efficiency across business operations. The cloud enables consistent innovation efforts, offering a strategic advantage and aid in remaining competitive in today's market. The cloud offers new methods to construct quick and adaptable solutions as organizations continue to grow and analyze data stockpiles. The way we approach, purchase, engage, and cooperate will keep evolving as new ideas arise.

GOING FOR CLOUD IS THE BEST DECISION FOR YOUR BUSINESS

Cost Efficient: Moving to the cloud saves the upfront cost of purchasing, managing and upgrading the IT systems. Thus using cloud model converts capital expenditure to operational expenditure. Using one-time-payment, 'pay as you go' model and other customized packages, organizations can significantly lower their IT costs.

Storage space: Businesses will no longer require file storage, data backup and software programs which take up most of the space as most of the data would be stored in remote cloud servers. Not only cloud frees in-house space but also provides unlimited space in the cloud.

Fault Resilient: While using own servers, you need to buy more hardware than you need in case of failure. In extreme cases, you need to duplicate everything. Moving to cloud eliminates redundancy and susceptibility to outages. Thus migrating to cloud not only adds reliability to the systems but also keeps information highly available.

Scalability: Using cloud computing, businesses can easily expand existing computing resources. For start-ups and growing enterprises, being able to optimize resources from the cloud enables them to escape the large one-off payments of hardware and software, making operational costs minimal.

Lean Management: With cloud, businesses can perform their processes more efficiently. Cloud migration leads existing workforce to focus on their core task of monitoring the infrastructure and improving them. Thus cloud computing leads to lean management and drives profitability.

Innovation: Innovation is directly tied to business growth. Using legacy technologies can hinder an organization's ability to both experiment with new solutions, and actually deploy those solutions at a scalable level. Fighting back-end performance issues can be a major struggle, especially in the realm of web applications. Using the cloud as an infrastructure base for innovation can lead to improved performance, lowered costs, and increased agility. For example, in the world of IoT product development, companies are driving innovation at a pace that's only possible through utilizing cloud computing. Cloud computing has enabled the IoT industry to innovate, create, and launch new products that are changing the world – and this applies across the entire tech ecosystem.

Enhanced Compliance & Security: Major cloud service providers are enterprise-level organizations that employ stringent security, compliance, and data protection standards. One of the main concerns business leaders have about cloud computing is transferring vital apps (as well as company and/or customer data) to the cloud. However, it's important to realize that all major cloud service providers dedicate vast amounts of resources to developing advanced security protocols, and follow strict regulatory/compliance requirements. Organizations that are in tightly-regulated industries such as healthcare, government, pharma, and defense, all need to follow countless industry-specific compliance requirements to ensure application and data integrity. Nearly all of the top organizations in these industries (and related verticals) are utilizing cloud computing services.

Flexibility: Flexibility is an oft-cited reason why cloud computing is important for business. Infrastructure is more flexible on the cloud – that much is obvious. However, flexibility also refers to cloud computing's inherently future-proof model. Tech is an ever-evolving industry – one where adaptation is not only needed for survival but is required for business growth. In the past, business expansion was a costly endeavor and one that typically involved dedicating large amounts of human and financial capital to one singular project (that may or may not end up generating business growth). Fast forward to today, and organizations have the technical ability to scale on-demand as the market changes. This on-demand flexibility of scaling capabilities is possible through the flexibility of cloud computing technology. Cloud computing's operational flexibility can be performed at a significantly lowered cost (compared to more traditionally resource-intensive methods).